# IMAGES OF WAR
# HITLER VERSUS STALIN:
# THE EASTERN FRONT 1942–1943

Soviet heavy artillery firing in support of Second Shock Army.

# IMAGES OF WAR
# HITLER versus STALIN:
# THE EASTERN FRONT 1942–1943
# STALINGRAD TO KHARKOV

RARE PHOTOGRAPHS FROM WARTIME ARCHIVES

NIK CORNISH

Pen & Sword
**MILITARY**

**This book is dedicated to my mum, Dorothy, to Liz and to our children, James, Charlotte and Alex**

First published in Great Britain in 2016 by
**PEN & SWORD MILITARY**
an imprint of
Pen & Sword Books Ltd,
47 Church Street, Barnsley,
South Yorkshire.
S70 2AS

ISBN 978-1-78346-399-2

A CIP catalogue record for this book is available
from the British Library

Typeset by Mac Style Ltd, Bridlington, East Yorkshire
Printed and bound in Great Britain by CPI

Pen & Sword Books Ltd incorporates the imprints of
Pen & Sword Aviation, Pen & Sword Family History, Pen & Sword Maritime,
Pen & Sword Military, Pen & Sword Discovery, Wharncliffe Local History,
Wharncliffe True Crime, Wharncliffe Transport, Pen and Sword Select,
Pen and Sword Military Classics

For a complete list of Pen & Sword titles please contact:
PEN & SWORD BOOKS LIMITED
47 Church Street, Barnsley, South Yorkshire, S70 2AS, England.
E-mail: enquiries@pen-and-sword.co.uk
Website: www.pen-and-sword.co.uk

# Contents

# Preface

The concept behind this book, and the others in the series, is to provide the general reader of military history with a heavily illustrated overview of the war on the Eastern Front between the years 1941 and 1945. Each book will be self-standing and cover a particular time period during this titanic four-year campaign.

There has never been war waged with such ferocity in the entirety of human history. It was indeed, as one eminent historian of this conflict entitled it, 'a clash of Titans'. On the one hand, the brown-shirted followers of Adolf Hitler, on the other, the red-flagged communists of Joseph Stalin. With two such totalitarian regimes where the power was highly concentrated in the hands of individuals who issued edicts through a vast civilian and military bureaucracy, the manner in which military and political advice was taken and acted upon frequently verged on the erratic.

As the spring of 1942 ushered in the thaw and then gave way to summer both Axis and Soviet forces once again squared up to one another. Neither side was able to mount operations on the scale of the previous year but nor were they were prepared to concede the initiative to the other. The period covered by this book includes operations from Crimea to the Caucasus and the suburbs of Leningrad. But the focus, inevitably, is on the grinding machine that was the Battle of Stalingrad and the battles of Army Group Centre which are sometimes overshadowed by the fighting on the Volga. The shattering of Army Group South did not spell its end, however, as events around Kharkov were to prove during the early months of 1943.

# Acknowledgements

The usual suspects to whom I am indebted include Dmitry Belanovsky, Norbert Hofer and Andrei Simonov – many thanks boys. Further thanks are due to Alex Cornish for many hours of technical assistance coupled with interesting comments and criticisms.

The debt that I owe to the staff members of the Central Museum of the Armed Forces and the Krasnogorsk Archive in Moscow is immense – thank you all.

**Picture Credits**

All images are by Nik Cornish at www.Stavka.org.uk aside from:

Courtesy of the Central Museum of the Armed Forces, Moscow via Stavka:
Frontispiece, p. x T, p. xi T, p. 6 B, p. 7 T, p. 12 B, p. 13 T, p. 24 T, p. 25, p. 30, p. 37 T, p. 53, p. 59 B, p. 76, p. 85 B, p. 86 B, p. 87 B, p. 88 B, p. 89 B, p. 90 B, p. 91 B, p. 98 T and B, p. 99 T, p. 101 T and B (right), p. 102 T, p. 103 B, p. 104 B, p. 109 B, p. 110 B, p. 112 T, p. 114 T, p. 115 T, p. 116 T, p. 117 T (right), p. 118 B, p.123 B, p. 124 B, p. 126 T, p. 127 B, p. 128 B, p. 129 B, p. 130 B, p. 131 B.

From the fonds of the RGAKFD in Krasnogorsk via Stavka:
p. 6 T, p. 13 B, p. 28 B, p. 29 T, p. 39 T, p. 105 B, p. 113 T, p. 116 B, p. 117 B, p. 118 T, p. 125 B.

# Introduction

From June 1941 to late March 1942 the western USSR as far to the east as Rostov on Don in the south, Moscow to the centre and Leningrad, the cradle of Bolshevism, had been the scene of fighting on an unprecedented scale. Three predominantly German forces, Army Group Centre (AGC), Army Group South (AGS) and Army Group North (AGN) had smashed their way to the very gates of the Soviet capital, briefly occupied Rostov on Don and besieged the isolated and starving Leningrad. The invading forces included contingents from Hungary, Finland, Slovakia, Italy and Romania.

The Red Army and the state it defended had been shaken to its very foundations. Air and tank fleets numbering tens of thousands of machines had been wiped from the balance sheet of forces, and millions of the USSR's soldiers had been killed, maimed or marched off to extemporized POW camps where they were to die of neglect or racial policy. The Soviet Union's breadbasket, Ukraine, east and west of the Dnieper River, was now a German fiefdom. The historic cities of Minsk and Smolensk were firmly under German control and the suburbs of Leningrad constituted its front line.

Apparently weakened beyond hope, with few if any infantry left, the Red Army had magicked men and materiel in sufficient quantities to first hold then drive back the might of AGC from the gates of Moscow. A combination of Soviet determination and courage when linked to the German's over-extended supply lines, high-command in-fighting and lack of a coherent plan all overshadowed by foul weather brought Operation Barbarossa to a halt. The New Year was ushered in by a Soviet offensive that succeeded in relieving the pressure along almost all the front line and drove the invaders back. This offensive then succumbed due to under resourcing, over ambitious objectives, German reinforcements and tenacity in defence.

From the northern and southern extremes in the Arctic, where the invasion had been halted short of its objective, and the Crimean Peninsula, where Sevastopol was under formal siege, a Soviet relief force languished bottled up in the Kerch Peninsula, both sides waited for their next set of orders from Berlin or Moscow. Each contender had been drained of human and other resources. Before the summer's operations began they would need to rebuild their forces and create more realistic plans that took into account their depleted armies.

With the spring thaw came the reminders of earlier fighting. Here a Soviet T 28 tank emerges from the ice and snow. How it was disabled is obvious.

Here a Finnish artillery piece is towed through the mud of the thaw. The gun is a 152mm M1909/30 piece captured from the Red Army. The Karelian Front was relatively quiet and both sides adopted positional warfare as the norm.

Aggressive patrolling was widespread as both sides jockeyed for positional and intelligence advantage. Here a group of Soviet infantry dash across the thaw-saturated ground.

Sometimes the only way the rations could reach the front was on horseback. Had man power been used the meal would have been cold on arrival.

Training recruits was a vital use of time for the Red Army as so many specialists had been lost during earlier campaigns.

Above the flooded land a wrecked and abandoned Soviet armoured train waits for a recovery team to make its way along the dyke-borne track.

Joseph Goebbels, Hitler's Propaganda Minister, seen here in Vienna during the summer of 1939, had become very much the face of the Nazi regime as Hitler reduced the number of public appearances he made. Goebbels was much concerned with the maintenance of civilian morale on the home front and encouraged the people to donate ski equipment and winter clothing to the troops on the Eastern Front. As Goebbels put it during his speech on the Führer's birthday (20 April 1942), 'We have come through a winter whose hardness and length have no equal in human history. It posed challenges to our leaders, to the front and to the homeland that we only now realize … An unbreakable band unites the front and the homeland.' As Hitler became more remote so Goebbels cultivated the image of the lone hero that the German *Volk* 'need only follow. His task is to show the way.'

# Chapter One

# Timoshenko's Failure

Modifying their plans after the failure of Operation Barbarossa took the Germans but little time. Recognizing that, despite reinforcements from both German and allied sources, the forthcoming campaigns would of necessity be less ambitious in scope. The target was both economic and political. In simple terms a line along the Volga River stretching from Astrakhan in the south, through Stalingrad then along the Don River to Voronezh, bending westwards towards Orel would form the eastern limit. However, it was to be the south east, into the Caucasus that the most important thrust would be made. The provinces of the Caucasus, stretching from the Kalmyk Steppe on the western shore of the Caspian Sea to the Kuban coastline along the eastern side of the Sea of Azov in the north to the borders with Turkey and Iran south of the Caucasus Mountains were rich in foodstuffs and oil. Economically Hitler wanted to control the oil and food production areas, politically he wished to draw Turkey into the war as an ally. To these ends the whole of AGS, commanded by Field Marshal von Bock, as well as the vast majority of the allied forces in the USSR would be committed. The plan was refined into several stages under the overall code name Operation Blau (Blue). To prepare the way Sevastopol and the Soviet position in the Kerch Peninsula were to be taken and the immense Soviet bridgehead over the Donets River at Izyum liquidated. With Crimea in Axis hands General Manstein's Eleventh Army would proceed north with its immense siege train to complete the destruction of Leningrad. In the wake of these operations on the flanks it was assumed, once again, that the Soviet empire would collapse and AGC roll forward to occupy Moscow.

For his part Stalin was equally ambitious. Plans had already been laid and infusions of support moved to the South Western Front (SW Front) and Southern Front (S Front) to provide weight for the upcoming attempt to liberate Kharkov and push on to the west. This operation was to begin on 12 May, when, so the meteorologists predicted, conditions would be ideal. But in the minds of Stavka (the Soviet high command) and Stalin the main German offensive would be directed towards Moscow and carried out by AGC. Stavka anticipated a thrust from the Rhzev Pocket, to the north of Moscow, with another from the south near Orel. These fears led to the accumulation of huge reserves along both the Bryansk Front and the Western Front (W Front). Discussions in Moscow were mainly concerned with the threat to Moscow but included reinforcing the Crimean Front in Kerch and breaking the siege lines around Leningrad. The build-up of AGS was studiously ignored. Still wedded to the concept of several partial offensives, the Soviets were to find out to their cost that intelligence reports were not only the products of fevered minds.

Marshal S.K. Timoshenko, effectively commanding both SW and S fronts, planned to destroy AGS and push westwards to the Dnieper River, south of Kiev, which was straightforward enough. Kharkov would be outflanked by two pincers: from the south Sixth Army, supported on its left by forces from the Izyum Bridgehead; from the north east Twenty-Eighth Army flanked by Twenty-First and Thirty-Eighth armies that would link up to the west of Kharkov. To prevent the Germans from moving reserves Bryansk Front's southern units would mount holding attacks in the Orel region. Unfortunately, the start of these operations had to be postponed until 16 May as fuel and food stocks were deemed too low. Consequently, when SW Front struck on 12 May co-ordination was lacking. Indeed, Timoshenko's offensive began six days prior to the jump-off date for AGS's attack on the Izyum Bridgehead.

Following a 60-minute artillery and aerial bombardment the Soviet armour and infantry attacks began. German Sixth Army, under General Paulus, bore the full fury of the offensive. To the north Twenty-First Army had established a 20km$^2$ bridgehead over the Donets River by the end of the first day. To the south progress was equally good. The Soviet report for that day noted '660 sorties' by aircraft that met very little opposition as the Luftwaffe's Fourth Air Fleet was directing its efforts against the Kerch Peninsula.

As the sun rose on 13 May the only clouds on the Soviet horizon were worrying intelligence reports of German armour and infantry gathering east of Kharkov. Nevertheless, the Soviets continued to advance throughout the morning. Despite stout resistance, Thirty-Eighth Army was soon within 18km of Kharkov. Moving as swiftly as they could, Soviet troops had no idea that they were being sucked into a trap. With midday just passed the Germans counterattacked. The 3rd and 23rd Panzer Divisions, with upwards of 300 tanks, crashed into the forward elements of Thirty-Eighth Army. Taken completely by surprise, the advance turned into a series of desperate rearguard actions as units fell back to stabilize the line. By the following day, Thirty-Eighth Army was reduced to a shambles, saved only by the advance of its armour that had been held in reserve. On the right flank Twenty-Eighth Army occupied a useful position but was unable to advance as German airstrikes smashed attack after attack before they started.

Operation Fridericus, the destruction of the Izyum Bridgehead, was now put in motion but in modified form.

One instead of two armoured forces would strike at the Izyum position from the south supported by every aircraft that could be spared from Crimea. Approved by Hitler and despite von Bock's last-minute apprehension, the offensive began on 17 May. By lunchtime the Axis forces had advanced some 17km into Ninth Army's lines and were thus in a position to threaten the rear of Fifty-Seventh Army. Both First Panzer and Seventeenth armies were now on the move, and 24 hours later the depth of penetration had quadrupled. Timoshenko, while warding off this threat, still pressed his armies towards Kharkov following a direct order from Stalin to do so. It was only on 19 May that the Kharkov attack was called off with Moscow's reluctant agreement. But, by that time, it was almost too late for Sixth and Fifty-Seventh armies as German Sixth Army threw its weight against the northern sector of the Izyum Bridgehead. To compound Soviet misery, no attacks were made elsewhere in an attempt to distract AGS. Poor communications and intelligence distribution had done little to help SW Front's units and it was often left up to the officers on the ground to decide what to do. Many such were well aware of the fate of Red Army soldiers, of all ranks, who did not perform as their last orders had dictated. Consequently, attacks and counterattacks were often launched into the teeth of certain death to avoid charges of disobedience later on.

As 20 May ended von Kleist and von Bock aimed to seal off the Izyum Bridgehead as swiftly as possible. Three days later the Axis jaws snapped shut around Sixth and Fifty-Seventh armies. However, these troops were in no mood to capitulate, and nor was Timoshenko going to leave them to their fate. Ordering attacks from within and without the pocket, SW Front's staff set about re-grouping their strength. Time, however, was not on the side of the Soviets. The Axis renewed its operations around the Izyum Bridgehead (known to the Germans as the Barvenkovo Pocket) with two objectives in mind. First, to hold off any relief attack and, secondly, to tighten the noose. The re-organized Thirty-Eighth Army was unable to prevent this or to mount a rescue attempt. Therefore, Sixth Army was forced to try and fight its way back down the road to Izyum.

The break-out began at 1000hr on 25 May. Amid scenes of carnage and slaughter the massed ranks of Soviet infantry pressed forward led by officers both military and political. At an untold cost in men, two German divisions were driven back until the human tide was stemmed by men of 1st Mountain Division. Wave after Soviet wave, guided by the eerie light of flares, battered away at the German machine-gun nests, but to no avail. Within the pocket the rear units of two armies were now inextricably mixed up in a confusion of men, animals and machines.

In such conditions it is no wonder that command structures ceased to function as the toll of dead officers reached astronomic proportions. By 26 May the survivors were jammed into a river valley measuring some 50km$^2$. Von Bock, who personally visited the ghastly scene, described it as 'overpowering' and still the Soviets would not surrender.

Timoshenko and his staff, making a similar front-line visit, spent almost the whole of 25 May sheltering from air attacks under a bridge. General A.M. Gorodinsky, commanding Sixth Army, died on the battlefield.

As night fell on 26 May break-out attempts continued with increasing ferocity supported by T 34s with infantry, fuelled, according to German accounts, by vodka. Desperate efforts by Thirty-Fifth Army to relieve the pressure met with little success owing to the power of the Fourth Air Fleet's Stukas. Nor were the attempts of S Front, attacking a weakened Seventeenth Army along the Mius River line that ran down to the Sea of Azov, any more effective in reducing the scale of the rapidly unfolding catastrophe.

From 27 May all cohesion in the pocket collapsed under a continual barrage. Here and there some units held together well enough to attempt a local break-out. Those that succeeded in breaking through the internal line were then faced with a march of up to 30km before reaching the front lines. Axis rear area security was, however, incomplete. Indeed, a force of 6 T 34s and roughly 20,000 men managed to escape by 28 May – the same day that Timoshenko ordered his forces over to the defensive and began to regroup to face the inevitable front-wide offensive that AGS was preparing to launch.

Calculating Soviet losses is always a difficult task. The currently accepted figures are over 270,000 casualties, of which 200,000 were taken prisoner. Losses of senior officers, experienced junior officers and NCOs were horrific as, during the last days of the pocket, many either committed suicide, died at the head of their men or fell into enemy hands. In just under three weeks SW Front had lost much of its combat effectiveness. Despite its losses, AGS was now the dominant force south of Moscow and Operation Blau's first objectives had been achieved.

An important part of AGS's strength was the contribution of Germany's allies. Although Hitler was not eager to share the laurels of victory, he was not averse to employing troops from other nations.

Hungary, with no grievance against the USSR, but wishing to retain control of Transylvania, had contributed what was known as the Mobile Corps to AGS in 1941. Impressed by the Hungarian's performance, the Germans requested an increase in their numbers. This took the form of Second Army and included an armoured formation. This force assembled near Kursk during June 1942. From the outset the Hungarians requested more powerful anti-tank guns than their 37mm types, which were ineffective against the majority of Soviet armour. The Hungarians formed part of the forces advancing towards Voronezh as, for historical and political reasons, it was inadvisable to position them near to the Romanians.

The latter, having regained the territory lost in 1940, maintained forces in Crimea and Ukraine. The Third and Fourth Romanian armies had been committed to Operation Barbarossa but Third Army was withdrawn to refit after the fall of Odessa. Brought up to a strength of over 350,000 men, the Romanian contingent was earmarked for the invasion of the Caucasus via the Kerch Peninsula and operations on the right flank of Sixth Army.

Nor was Mussolini anxious to be left out. The CSIR (the Italian Expeditionary Corps in Russia) had not performed well during the recent winter but, during March 1942, II Army Corps, the Alpine Corps and several para-military Blackshirt units were sent to the USSR. Numbering over 225,000 men, these units were re-designated Eighth Army and marched east to positions north of Stalingrad. Their cavalry arm was notable as it carried out one of the last mounted charges in history on 24 August 1942.

The other noteworthy additions to AGS' strength were the Slovakians and the Croatians. Slovakia's Mobile Division, its main contribution, had earned itself a good reputation in 1941 and cemented this during its time with First Panzer Army. Croatia's puppet ruler sent a three-battalion force known as the Croatian Legion, or the 369th Reinforced Croat Infantry Regiment.

However, these allied contingents were, without exception, poorly equipped for the modern, mobile war they were involved in. Despite such shortcomings, during the early weeks of the next phase of Operation Blau they were to make a very useful contribution as the rapid advance across the steppes was to show. Before the main offensive began, regrouping and reinforcement was necessary and there was also the situation in Crimea to resolve.

To encourage Stalin and Stavka to believe that the Axis summer offensive would target Moscow POWs were, during the spring, asked specific questions regarding the capital's defences. Reconnaissance flights over the area were stepped up and on 29 May the high command ordered 'the earliest possible resumption of the attack on Moscow' by AGC. This deception was known as Operation Kremlin.

German paratroopers board their transport on 15 May to be dropped on Ternovaia as reinforcements for isolated units defending this vital position. Some 300 men were dropped that day followed by others 4 days later.

Soviet infantry mounted on T 34 tanks ride into action during May 1942. Tank *desant* troops (infantry carried into battle riding on tanks) were a solution to the Red Army's lack of armoured personnel carriers. Travelling on the back of a tank of a vehicle moving at more than 25km per hour under fire would have done little to calm the nerves generated by going into battle.

Tractors move forward towing heavy artillery during the fighting around Kharkov. Soviet analysts later commented that the lack of such weapons made the task of reducing German hedgehog positions almost impossible thus slowing the advance. Fear of Luftwaffe attack is highlighted by the mass of camouflaged materiel.

Armed with a captured German MG 34, this Soviet soldier is supporting an attack. Infantry tactics were often primitive, attempting to overrun positions by weight of numbers rather than guile. Subsequently, casualties were heavy.

Soviet armour was committed too late to hold up the Operation Fridericus and prevent the Axis from gaining the initiative. Once again experienced panzer troops overwhelmed the still poorly trained Red Army crews.

The figures returned by SW Front for the period 10–31 May reported that Sixth Soviet Army and attached units losses included 468 tanks, 2,600 guns and mortars and almost 150,000 men. Here a KV-1 is inspected by a German mountain soldier.

Another column of Soviet POWs makes its way westwards.

Hungary's contribution to AGS included First Cavalry Brigade. These troopers are part of the unit's machine-gun section. Well-mounted and the heirs to a long tradition, they performed well during the summer of 1942.

A Toldi light tank of the Hungarian armoured division sent to join AGS in spring 1942. Although equipped with various types of non-domestic armour, the crews were poorly trained in armoured warfare. Nevertheless, they acquitted themselves well at the Battle of Uryv, July 1942, when they destroyed twenty-one T 34s without loss.

To the right, the first commander of the Croatian Legion, Colonel Ivan Markulj. Markulj led the unit until May 1942 when he returned to Croatia to take up administrative duties. The red and white chequered arm shield of the Croatian force is clearly visible on his arm.

Italian alpine troops, wearing their distinctive *Cappello Alpini* headgear and plus-four breeches. This elite corps was formed of three divisions. They participated in the advance to the Don River. Oddly, they were ill-equipped for cold weather warfare despite their speciality being mountain operations.

A captain of the North Caucasian Legion, a unit raised in early 1942 from POWs and deserters who enlisted to fight the Soviets. The officer has been awarded the Eastern People's Decoration for Merit. When AGS advanced across the Don Steppe and into the Caucasus the flow of volunteers increased dramatically.

Romania's military commitment was by far the largest made to AGS. Two of the newly arrived infantry divisions, 1st and 4th, were badly mauled during the fighting of May 1942 due to their inexperience. Over 380,000 Romanian troops were allotted to this sector of the front.

Mounted on a T 60 chassis this BM-8 multi-barrelled rocket launcher was one of the Katyusha family. Deployed with Guards Mortar units, they were a rarely taken prize.

Soviet gunners check their co-ordinates. The black branch of service patch on the enlisted man's collar can be clearly seen as can the senior lieutenant's rank insignia.

Patrolling and securing the vast rivers of southern Russia was a task best carried out cautiously. As the only defensible lines facing the Axis advance, it was essential all fords and bridges were well-guarded.

The vast steppes offered little in the way of cover for armoured or infantry attacks. Following up a group of tank *desant* men riding on a T 34, Soviet riflemen run through the dust. The nationality of the aircraft is unknown.

# Chapter Two

# The Iron Fortress

The city and port of Sevastopol are situated on the northern shore of a peninsula on the western coast of Crimea. The port opens onto Severnaya Bay which is fed by the Chernaya River, the banks of which, to the east of the city, were marshy in 1942. Sevastopol's defence line ran in an arc from the south of the Belbek River in the north to slightly east of Balaclava port in the south at the base of the peninsula. The distance from city to defence line ranged from 10–15km and ran for 37km. A second line, 5km from the city, had also been prepared by civilian labour. The entire area was divided into four sectors, numbered from 1–4 anti-clockwise from Balaclava. Almost every defensive position was within range of Eleventh Army's heavy artillery. The Soviets had dug in on every ridge and hillock, liberally sown mines of all types and entrenched wherever tactically useful. Backing the infantry were the heavy guns of the coastal batteries and the vast concrete and armour plate structures of the forts, turreted gun emplacements that resembled nothing less than land battleships. These positions would prove incredibly difficult to neutralize, particularly when ably defended by their garrisons and gun crews.

With roughly 100,000 men, the majority of whom were sailors, the Soviet commanders were short of ammunition for the large number of guns, over 400 that they deployed. Nevertheless, they were optimistic that they could hold out as supply ships continued to make their way through the porous blockade.

Operation Storfang (Sturgeon Catch), the third assault on Sevastopol, was planned in meticulous detail. Short of infantry, Manstein could not afford the profligate tactics of earlier operations. Infantry assault groups, including flamethrower armed pioneers, amply supplied with grenades and wire cutters, would spearhead the attacks. The aerial and artillery support was on a lavish scale including gigantic 600mm 'Karl' mortars and von Richthofen's VIII Fliegerkorps' seventy-three Stuka ground-attack aircraft and other bombers. The XXX Army Corps was to make small attacks towards Balaclava which were intended to pin Soviet reserves while LIV Army Corps, to the north facing the Belbek River and the main Soviet fortresses and coastal artillery batteries, would launch the principal, breakthrough attack. This army corps would enjoy the support of the greater part of the siege guns. In the centre of the Axis line lay the Romanian Mountain Corps that could be called upon to provide supporting infantry attacks as their artillery branch was negligible.

Aware that his air assets would be withdrawn to support AGS' offensive, Manstein was under pressure to conclude the offensive in the shortest time possible. Therefore, the Soviets would be subjected to a colossal bombardment from the air and the land to begin on 2 June.

When the guns began their work at 0540hr they followed a carefully prepared fire plan targeting specific locations to conserve ammunition. The Luftwaffe joined in 20 minutes later. During the course of the next five days the bombardment increased in intensity with the heavier guns concentrating on the positions covering the Belbek River. Soviet counterbattery fire was minimal to prevent their positions being located and to conserve ammunition.

Finally, at 0425hr on 7 June, elements of LIV Army Corps attacked as the last shells of the final barrage impacted. The objective was the link position between Defence Sectors 3 and 4. Several key positions and, by the end of 8 June, some 15km$^2$ of territory had been overrun but at no little cost in men and munitions. Then followed three days of small actions, as each side realigned, which preceded a major Soviet counterattack that aimed to restore the entire position. Unfortunately for the Soviet naval infantry involved, they made progress due to the Luftwaffe's mastery of the skies which allowed Fliegerkorps VIII to strafe any attack into bloody oblivion. As this attempt staggered to its hopeless conclusion it became obvious that the Belbek River position was rapidly becoming untenable.

The capture of Fort Stalin on 13 June led to another period of reorganization lasting for four days. This was followed by 36 hours of attack and counterattack interspersed with artillery and aerial fire which finally drove the Soviets back to the shores of Severnaya Bay other than some isolated units. Defence Sector 4 was now in ruins and Sector 3 on the verge of collapse.

To the south XXX Army Corps had made modest initial progress, and this improved dramatically when a Soviet unit exchange was interrupted and a 2km breach forced open. But, as the third week of June began, XXX Army Corps was running out of steam. Therefore, the Romanians were ordered into action. By 25 June they had broken into Soviet positions east of the Chernaya River.

However, such slow advances and the impending departure of Fliegerkorps VIII led Manstein to order an attack across Severnaya Bay with a simultaneous attack on the Sapun Ridge by XXX Army Corps.

The Severnaya Bay water-borne attack achieved rapid success during the night of 28/29 June. Soviet confusion led to the loss of key high ground and a degree of panic along the line. Similar German achievements at Sapun Ridge presaged a collapse of both Soviet flanks and a poorly controlled withdrawal on Sevastopol began. At 0950hr on 30 June Stalin ordered the city abandoned and that senior Party and military leaders be evacuated as a matter of priority. Chaos, disillusion and panic resulted in wounded soldiers being trampled by Party personnel and hangers-on in a desperate attempt to leave.

On the morning of 1 July the first German flag was raised over Sevastopol and within four days the remaining pockets of resistance were extinguished, any survivors fleeing to join the partisans in the hills south east of the city. Sevastopol was firmly in Axis hands and Eleventh Army prepared to move to join AGC as AGS marched towards the Volga and its destiny.

The winter had, apparently, ended operations in the Arctic region. But, on 1 January 1942, the Soviets attacked across a front stretching from Kriv to Maaselka Station on the Murmansk–Leningrad railway line. Breaking through at the town of Kriv, the Red Army created a bulge that threatened the Finnish railhead at Karhumaki and forces at Poventsa to the east with encirclement. However, a timely counterattack on 12 January broke through the base of the Soviet position and cut off the forces closing on the railhead. Hard fighting in atrocious conditions resulted in the Finns re-establishing their position prior to the Soviet attack. As was the way of operations in this central section of the front, the forces involved were few in number, rarely numbering more than a brigade or two. Indeed, the Finns interrupted traffic on the Murmansk railway using two battalions that undertook a 150km round-trip raid that destroyed the station at Maj-Guba.

To the south Finland's policy of not escalating their involvement much beyond the restoration of the 1939 border continued. In early 1942 100,000 men of the Karelian Army were demobilized and Marshal Mannerheim, Finland's Commander-in-Chief, dismissed German requests to put pressure on the Soviet positions guarding Leningrad's northern flanks. However, the Finns did participate in the capture of two islands in the Gulf of Finland – Gogland and Tyuters, both of which fell during late March. These successes were overshadowed by the Soviet Spring Offensive. In an attempt to extend the buffer zone around Murmansk before the thaw set in the Red Army attacked on 24 April. Specialist ski-troops, supported by a battalion of tanks, broke through Finnish III Army Corps en route to Kestenga. This was followed by a sea-borne assault on the German 6th Division's position by Soviet marines. Unfortunately for the Soviets, their early progress came to nothing. The 8th Ski Brigade lost momentum in swamps north of Kestenga where its men were slaughtered and the marines re-embarked on 14 May. A week later the Finns counterattacked but took several days to crack the well-built and cleverly placed defence line. This operation, again to German chagrin, was called off on 23 May. Despite receiving a full rifle division by way of reinforcement, the Soviets did not mount any serious operations, and in fact these men did little more than replace the casualties suffered.

The fighting, both in the front line and, politically, in the rear had damaged Finno-German relations badly, highlighting the differences in their war aims. From the White Sea to the Gulf of Finland the situation became very much akin to immobile, positional warfare. It underwent little change until 1944, by which time the men on both sides had made themselves as comfortable as possible in the vile conditions that the environment generated.

Leningrad, under siege since late 1941, was, so Hitler decided, to be left to be starved into submission. However, Stalin was resolved that the siege lines be broken and the tormented population relieved. The major attempt of early 1942 had begun on 4 January, and by late February AGN's forces were in a critical position. But, on 15 March, the situation changed dramatically as a result of a well-executed German counterstroke that virtually decapitated the Soviet incursion into their lines, culminating in the isolation of Second Shock Army. So heavy were the Red Army's losses, in the region of over 400,000 men, that operations ceased in March 1942.

One month later Hitler issued his Führer Directive 41 that included an order to capture not besiege Leningrad. AGN was told that it would be suitably reinforced to carry out this mission during the summer. AGN's commander *General Feld Marschall* Kuchler's staff devised three plans. Operation Beggar's Staff aimed at crushing the coastal enclave around Oranienbaum, west of Leningrad, and Operation Moor Fire to eliminate the Pogot'se Salient. These two were deemed achievable with AGN's current resources. It was the third, Operation Northern Light, the capture of Leningrad, that would require the arrival of Eleventh Army's assets from the Crimea.

From late April until the end of June AGN was heavily engaged eliminating the isolated Second Shock Army. Nor were the Soviets completely quiescent, frequently attacking Sixteenth Army's positions during June and July. Nor did it help AGN that Stavka was well aware of Operation Northern Light and determined to hold Leningrad at all costs. Hitler, in late July, decreed that the city should be taken by early September that year.

The fall of Sevastopol freed Eleventh Army and its attendant siege artillery but the condition of its men and materiel left much to be desired. Nor did AGN have the resources to carry out operations Beggar's Staff and Moor Fire. Kuchler convinced Hitler that both should be postponed until Leningrad had fallen. Consequently, when elements of Eleventh Army began to shuffle north during August, there was no apparent need for haste as the offensive was timed to begin on 14 September. When Manstein arrived at AGN, on 27 August, his force was not placed under AGN's control but that of OKH, and, furthermore, he was given full responsibility for the execution of Operation Northern Light. Meanwhile, Kuchler was using units of his own plus those of Eleventh Army to shore up AGN's defences as a Soviet offensive was getting underway. Leningrad Front's Fifty-Fifth Army had established a bridgehead on the German-held bank of the Neva River and Volkhov Front, east of the city, was pushing its Eighth Army towards it. Although the Soviet fronts got to within 8km of each other, the German lines held. Assembling more and more of Eleventh Army, Kuchler gathered his forces around Siniavino and, on 1 September, counterattacked in strength. By 12 September the situation was restored but despite this Manstein was now in overall command. The first German attacks failed but the second series cut off the main bodies of Eighth Army and the reformed Second Shock Army. A diversionary attack from the Neva Bridgeheads failed to achieve anything but the postponement of the inevitable. Between 30 September and 15 October the encircled men of Volkhov Front's armies were ground down but most of the infantry managed to escape without their heavy equipment. Meretskov, Volkhov Front's commander, was forbidden further attacks and ordered to assume a defensive stance. But by now it was clear that Operation Northern Light was a non-starter. On 14 October Manstein was also ordered to dig in. Now Hitler reverted to the idea of destroying Leningrad's defences with artillery fire prior to a renewal of Operation Northern Light at some indeterminate point in the future. Manstein was to remain with AGN until 20 November when he was ordered south to restore the situation to the rear of Sixth Army. Whether or not AGN would have taken Leningrad is a moot point even with the support of additional artillery and aerial assets. During October Govorov, commanding Leningrad Front, and Meretskov started planning their next offensive. The first priority was to rebuild their decimated forces. The defences in and around the city itself had been further developed and strengthened, reinforcements arriving in significant numbers via Lake Ladoga throughout the autumn and simultaneously Volkhov Front steadily increased its numbers. The new offensive was due to begin early in 1943 coinciding with operations further south.

Turret number 2 of Coastal Battery 30 following its capture. The turret was displaced by a close miss from one of the 'Karl' 600mm mortars, on 6 June. The guns seen here are 305mm pieces.

150mm Nebelwerfer 41 batteries were used in large numbers during the final assault on Sevastopol. Organized in batteries of six launchers, the Germans deployed nine such batteries. They were more effective than the vastly more expensive and complicated super heavy artillery.

The more effective 'bunker busters' employed by the Eleventh Army were the sixteeen 305mm, Skoda mortars. A pre-First World War design, it remained in production until 1943.

The majority of the ground troops employed by the Soviets were naval men. They underwent rudimentary infantry training, as seen here, during early 1942. They were to prove tough and resilient opponents for the *landser*. They wore their distinctive naval uniforms throughout the siege as a matter of honour.

Soviet infantry launch a counterattack during mid-June 1942. Often such operations were poorly timed due to disrupted communications or poor intelligence.

The German operational map photographed at an Axis press briefing during Operation Storfang.

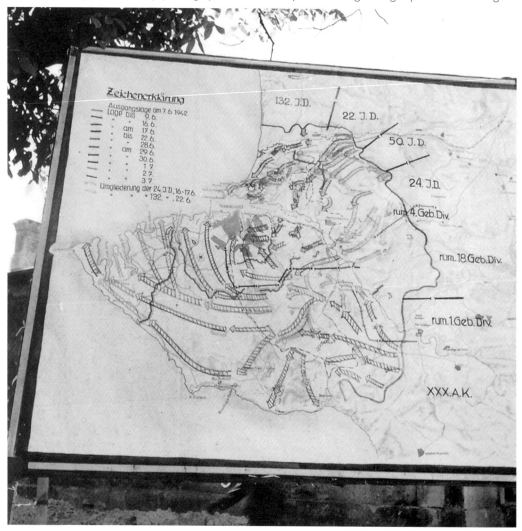

Crossing Severnaya Bay was carried out under cover of a smokescreen and in boats such as those seen here. Speed and surprise were vital and resulted in low German casualties despite the risks involved.

The number of POWs taken during the last weeks of fighting at Sevastopol was tiny when compared with the previous year's bag. The final days of the Soviet defence were marred by a scramble for evacuation led by senior officers and Party *apparatchiks* (Communist Party functionaries).

An unnamed Soviet defence position facing XXX Army Corps north of Balaclava. Given the lack of camouflage, it is possibly a line hastily thrown together as an emergency measure to hold up pursuers.

Triumphant but exhausted, smiling German infantry in Sevastopol's port area. However, such had been the severity of the final offensive that Eleventh Army's infantry were granted an extended period of rest before transferring to AGN for the reduction of Leningrad.

Soviet ski-troops on patrol. Frequently these men encountered marshes and rock-strewn ground that rendered their specialist skills useless.

Be it German, Russian or Finnish, the order banning smoking in the latrines was strictly enforced.

Age-old transport methods still proved reliable in the wintry conditions north of Leningrad as this Red Army supply column demonstrates.

One of the earliest examples of foreign aid to the USSR was this Hurricane Mk 1. These aircraft served on the Arctic Front with mixed success, as seen here. Some Hurricanes, British aid from the Winter War, were to be found in Finnish hands.

An officer of one of Northern Fleet's fifteen submarines watches the surface. A K-21 submarine, commanded by Captain N.A. Lunin, unsuccessfully attacked the *Tirpitz* in June 1942. As well as conducting patrols submarines were used to land troops behind enemy lines.

The Finnish Air Force had licence-built some forty-five Blenheim Mk I aircraft prior to 1939. They remained in service during the Continuation War until 1945. The blue swastika was the marking of the Finnish Air Force from 1918 until 1944. The Finns did not bomb civilian targets or overfly Soviet bases to avoid provocation and spare valuable machines.

The German gunners' view of Leningrad was accurate as well as frustrating bringing the prize into clear sight.

German medical staff at a hospital established at the Tsar's former palace complex at Tsarskoe Selo (renamed Pushkin by the Bolsheviks), 24km south of central Leningrad.

When Lake Ladoga froze sufficiently, during the winter of 1941–2, lorries were able to cross it, although not without risk. Named the 'Road of Life' by the city's population, this made a vital contribution to the people's survival by evacuating them and bringing in supplies.

Across the city extemporized workshops for weapons maintenance and production sprang up. Here a worker checks a PPD 40 sub-machine gun. Forerunner of the PPSh, it was less crudely made and featured the signature drum magazine.

Mountain troops of Eleventh Army arrive behind the front during the summer of 1942. They were to be used to take Leningrad but instead became involved in the defensive battles then raging.

Soviet heavy artillery firing in support of Second Shock Army. The weapon seen here is a 152mm M 1937 howitzer. The tube is at its maximum elevation of 65 degrees. The rate of fire, in the hands of a well-trained crew, was four rounds per minute.

# Chapter Three

# To the Volga

Having achieved the two prerequisites necessary before the opening of the summer campaign in the southern USSR, the elimination of the Barvenkovo Salient and the occupation of Sevastopol, the ground was clear for AGS to begin its offensive.

An incomplete copy of the plans for Operation Blau had fallen into Soviet hands on 17 June. However, it was dismissed by Stalin as a ruse as he was convinced that Moscow remained Germany's priority. At this time Soviet planning was focused on an operation designed to liberate Orel involving Western and Bryansk fronts.

AGS was under the command of Field Marshal von Bock and numbered approximately 1,000,000 German and 300,000 allied troops. Additional armoured units had been contributed by AGN and AGC with air support in the form of Luftflotte IV under Colonel General Richthofen. The objectives of Operation Blau, renamed Operation Braunschweig (Brunswick) as a result of the loss of the plans, were simple but long-ranging. The first stage consisted of Second and Fourth Panzer armies advancing on the vital transport hub of Voronezh on the Don River, roughly halfway between Moscow and Stalingrad. Stage two involved Sixth Army, operating east of Kharkov, enveloping Soviet formations west of the upper Don River and south of Voronezh. With the completion of these missions Fourth Panzer Army would turn south and, following the encirclement of Stalingrad, join Seventeenth Army on the banks of the Volga River. Then would begin the fourth stage – the offensive that would secure the Caucasian oil fields and the granary of the Kuban Steppe for the Axis. Stalingrad was, without doubt, at this point a secondary target.

In accepted Blitzkrieg fashion Operation Braunschweig began on 28 June at 0600hr with 24th Panzer Division advancing hard as the echoes of the last explosions of bomb and shell had died away towards the Kshen River. Stavka's reaction was to order tank units to converge around Voronezh to meet this thrust. As 24th Panzer expanded into the gap between Thirteenth and Fortieth armies it overran the latter's HQ at Kastornoye, 60km west north west of Voronezh. Golikov, commanding Bryansk Front, was refused permission to pull back the left wing of Fortieth Army. However, the situation was developing very badly for the Soviets and on 1 July Bryansk Front was given permission to withdraw its left. This move coincided with SW Front's withdrawal of its right wing for, by now, Sixth Army had commenced its attack on SW Front. Here the situation was rapidly becoming disastrous for Timoshenko's men, already weakened by the events of May.

The penetration by AGS into SW and Bryansk fronts' line had expanded into a salient of 240km wide by 130km deep. The rear areas of both SW and Southern fronts were now in jeopardy and Voronezh was directly threatened. During the night 3/4 July IIL Panzer Corps crossed the Don River west of the city. At this point Voronezh Front was created to plug the hole between Bryansk and SW fronts. Meanwhile, to the south First Panzer Army was rolling towards the Donets River and proceeding in a north-easterly direction just as Sixth Army was south east from Rossosh: a vast encirclement in the Don River bend seemed the obvious aim.

As the fighting for Voronezh raged Stavka indulged in an orgy of self-criticism, condemnation and new appointments. With Voronezh, Rostov on Don and Stalingrad now under threat it was clear that Moscow was not on the agenda. Therefore, Stalin and his advisors reconsidered the situation. The 40-year-old General N.F. Vatutin took command of Voronezh Front and Timoshenko was placed at the head of the newly created Stalingrad Front on 12 July. The latter consisted of Sixty-Second and Sixty-Fourth armies with elements of other formations along with Eighth Air Army. In addition, Sixty-Third Army formed part of the screen covering Stalingrad. These units were to act as backstop for units of SW Front that were retreating towards the north of Stalingrad. Stavka had issued orders six days earlier that authorized withdrawal rather than encirclement. Additionally, reserve formations, held to protect Moscow, were now on the move to the south. As these alterations fell into place, SW Front's retreat continued apace while desperate fighting in and around Voronezh obliged von Bock to retain Fourth Panzer Army to upset any serious counterattacks. Voronezh, as well as tying up German forces, was vitally important as it protected the Tambov–Saratov rail and river transport network. Through this region flowed oil and other vital strategic resources from the south and east. It was also a major north–south rail link. Indeed, with this rail link under air attack many of the reserves moving south were forced to undertake long marches that sapped their energy and cost valuable time. Despite vicious combat, Voronezh fell on 9 July but it was too late for Hitler who replaced von Bock with Field Marshall Weichs. This was one of the first acts the Führer carried out that led to the modification of Operation Braunschweig. On 10 July AGS was re-organized into Army Groups A and B (AGA and AGB). AGA would consist of Seventeenth Army, and First Panzer and Fourth Panzer armies as well as Third Romanian Army. AGB comprised Sixth Army, Second Hungarian, Eighth Italian and Fourth Romanian armies – a truly representative Axis force.

AGA was to advance from its current position, capture Rostov and occupy the western shore of the Black Sea as far south as Batum near the Turkish border, as well as the oil-production areas at Grozny and Maikop and the Caspian Sea coast down to Baku – an incredibly tall order by any stretch of the imagination. Seventeenth and Third Romanian armies would comprise the right flank while First Panzer and Fourth Panzer armies the left. The Caucasian offensive was known as Operation Edelweiss.

To the north, as the Italians and Hungarians took up defensive positions along the front from Voronezh southwards, Sixth Army, less XL Panzer Corps en route to Rostov, would move on Stalingrad.

Stalingrad was in its way as much of a symbol of communist Russia as were Moscow and Leningrad. It was there during the Russian Civil War that Stalin, as military Commissar, had forged the bonds with Voroshilov, Timoshenko and Buddeny that were to guide Soviet military affairs until 1942. The city was built and expanded along the western bank of the Volga River. It was a centre of heavy industry, much of which had been turned over to munitions production including armour and artillery. It was placed on a war footing on 19 July 1942. Civilians, indeed almost 50 per cent of the 500,000 population, were marched off to build defences and dig anti-tank ditches. In addition, 11,000 men were recruited to form 'Annihilation Battalions' to protect strategic positions against German paratroopers and supplementing the 'Worker's Battalions' already mustered. There were no bridges over the Volga River at Stalingrad but its position dominated this vital north–south artery and it also covered some of the last remaining rail lines connecting these points. Thus, it had more than symbolic value to both Stalin and Hitler.

AGB, now effectively reduced to Sixth Army, began its attack on Stalingrad on 22–3 July across a 200km front. Within hours Sixty-Third Army was in danger of an outflanking move to the north and Sixty-Fourth Army was in a similarly precarious position as their junction was under threat. An attempt to shore up the junction point utilizing a mixed force of marines and armour between the Chir and Don rivers failed utterly. Another attempt involving First and Fourth Tank armies (formerly Twenty-Eighth and Thirty-Eighth armies and both in dreadful condition) was timed to start on 27 July. Under continual air attack these troops crawled forwards. On 31 July Hitler instructed Fourth Panzer Army to support the drive on Stalingrad.

To counter this threat General V. I. Chuikov, commander of Sixty-Fourth Army, took charge of a scratch force defending the Aksai River while Stavka created South Eastern Front (SE Front) under General A.I. Yeremenko which was to control the southern section of Stalingrad's defences. However, in the field matters had taken a critical turn for the worse. To decapitate a serious German penetration of Sixty-Second Army, First and Fourth Tank armies, now reduced to thirty tanks between them, had failed in their attack resulting in a significant part of Sixty-Second Army being encircled on 9 August. Now the fate of the city was in the balance. Stalin therefore committed his command team of last resort, generals Zhukov and Vassilevsky, to the south with orders to report directly to him.

The defence rings around Stalingrad were from outer to inner Line O, Line K, Line S and Line G, which lay within the city itself. On 15 August the last Soviet bridgeheads on the western shore of the Don River were overrun. By 23 August 16th Panzer Division had crossed a hastily constructed pontoon bridge in support of its advancing infantry to consolidate a 10km$^2$ enclave. Despite artillery and aerial bombardment the German position held firm and the build-up for the drive on the city began.

Hitler had ordered Paulus to take the city a little more than a month earlier in the following manner, 'occupy the town and block the land communications between Don and the Volga ...'. Just a few days after that announcement Stalin had issued an equally if not more savage instruction, 'it is time to finish retreating ... panic mongers and cowards should be exterminated in place ...'. The 16th Panzer Division covered 80km reaching the northern suburb of Stalingrad, Spartanovka, just before midnight on 23 August. Covering the city was a pall of smoke from the burning oil storage tanks along the river bank.

When Stalin received news that the Germans were on the banks of the Volga he was incandescent. However, the final line of his orders to Yeremenko was positive, 'the most important thing is not to let panic take hold, do not be afraid of the enemy thrusts and keep your faith in our ultimate success'. Later that night he spoke with Yeremenko and denied him permission to evacuate any industrial concerns. Thus was the Red Army committed to fight for Stalingrad with its back to the broad Volga River.

Daily, from 23 August, the Luftwaffe rained down bombs on the city. The following day a counterattack by Sixty-Second Army failed and Sixty-Second and Sixty-Fourth armies fell back to defence lines K and S. Factory militiamen were ordered to turn their places of work into fortresses and barricade streets. On 27 August Zhukov was promoted to Deputy Supreme Commander, answerable only to Stalin himself and ordered south. His task was to co-ordinate an attack by Twenty-Fourth, First Guards and Sixty-Sixth armies to relieve the pressure on Stalingrad Front's northern sector. Under-gunned and poorly equipped, First Guards and Twenty-Fourth armies attacked during the first week of September but achieved little, by which time Sixty-Second and Sixty-Fourth armies were manning the final defence line. By 12 September Stalingrad Front was in position along Line G inside the city itself. As the Soviet attacks to the north continued Sixth Army positioned itself for what it believed would be the *coup de grâce*.

On 10 September Chuikov was named commander of Sixty-Second Army by Yeremenko and N.S. Kruschev Stalingrad Front's Political Commissar. One of his first tasks was to consider the defences which, despite the number of workers committed to them, were less than half finished. On 12 September Paulus and Zhukov reported to their respective overlords. Whereas Paulus appraised Hitler of his plans to capture Stalingrad, Zhukov and Vassilevsky had begun to organize the operation that they hoped would smash the German positions by simultaneous attacks on the weak Axis forces on Sixth Army's flanks. But for that to succeed Stalingrad would have to be held at any price.

General Friedrich Paulus, commander of Sixth Army, was described by his former commander General Heinz Guderian as 'brilliantly clever, conscientious, hardworking, original and talented'. His promotion to Field Marshal was the last dispatch received by his HQ 2 hours before he surrendered on 31 January 1943.

The view from the nose of a Heinkel 111 approaching Stalingrad. The Luftwaffe struck deep behind Soviet lines, playing havoc with units moving across the open steppe. Air superiority was a vital component of the Axis' advance during the summer of 1942.

A BA-10 armoured car lies abandoned near Fortieth Army's HQ. Many of these vehicles were used by the Axis in a security role. Armed with two machine guns and a 45mm gun, it was a solid, reliable vehicle but, by 1943, had been phased out of Soviet service.

T 34s roar across the steppe near Voronezh, part of the seven tank corps committed to the counterattack. Such efforts often failed due to poor intelligence and communications.

German armour, Panzer IIIs of Fourth Panzer Army, moves carefully into the western suburbs of Voronezh, 5 July 1942.

With what appears to be Voronezh railway station to his rear, a German NCO poses for a photo. The city fell too late to save von Bock's career.

In threatened areas across southern Russia thousands of civilians were mobilized to dig defences. Here one such group puts the finishing touches to a gun position.

By the summer of 1942 Soviet troops were becoming more effective at dealing with German armour. Here an anti-tank gun crew, in text book formation, undergoes basic training. The gun seen here is an M1937 45mm piece, served by a four-man crew.

Panic ensued when the Luftwaffe struck at the Soviet units falling back on the confluence of the Chir and Don rivers on 25 July. As one observer wrote, 'A mass of men and vehicles rushed towards the Don.' The result is obvious from this image.

Although mostly obscured by the censor's pencil, the markings of 11th Panzer Division can just be seen. This formation was part of Fourth Panzer Army. The men's immaculate appearance is something of a contrast with front-line troops nearer the 'sharp end'.

Soviet infantry prepare to launch another counterattack north of Stalingrad.

Abandoned Soviet defences, including the bunker in the foreground and the anti-tank ditch towards the top left. A German supply column can be seen driving alongside the latter. There is little or no sign of fighting.

Carrying a load of infantry, a Panzer III raises dust as the advance towards the Volga continues.

Looking tanned, well-fed and healthy, German artillerymen make ready their 105mm light field howitzer. This is the earlier version without the range-increasing muzzle brake that was fitted from March 1942 onwards.

During the summer of 1942 POWs were rarer than during the previous summer's campaigns now that the Soviets were prepared to trade space for time. Civilians were often left to their own devices and chose to remain at home with their herds and flocks.

Spotting for the artillery could be a hazardous task and therefore maximum concealment was essential.

The inner defence line often consisted of rubble barricades, which would provide little defence against much more than small arms fire. The effects of round-the-clock Luftwaffe activity can be seen from the burned out shells of the buildings in the background.

Clutching their few possessions, survivors of the bombing emerge from their cellar shelters into the summer sunshine following an early air raid on Stalingrad. Images such as this were circulated to stiffen the resolve of the Red Army.

# Chapter Four

# Into the Caucasus

AGA's operations towards Rostov on Don, the so-called 'Gateway to the Caucasus', had been less spectacular than the attacks of its sister formation, AGB. The advance, underway since early July, had not netted the massive bag of POWs that had been the norm the previous year. Covered by well-led rearguard actions, the Soviet retirement had been carried out efficiently. On 25 July Rostov fell along with the vitally important bridge over the Don River. It had taken two days of ferocious house-to-house fighting to secure the city as far as the river. Fanatically defended by NKVD troops, building after bloody building had to be dealt with before the second bridge, at Bataisk, was taken. The bridgeheads held firm in the face of fierce counterattacks and it now remained for AGA to realign itself for the push into the Caucasus and the economic prizes that glittered on the far horizon.

Ominously, German intelligence reports were noting a more determined, professional approach to war than had previously been the case. Indeed, a senior German officer witnessed the 'Russians asserting their old mastery in rearguard fighting'. Tenacity in defence and tactical modernization were to prove key elements in the coming months.

Field Marshal List, commander of AGA, 24 hours after the fall of Rostov, identified that the overarching concern about the offensive into the Caucasus was not so much the opposition but the immense problem of supplying more than twenty-five divisions moving towards widely divergent objectives to the south west and south east. Von Kleist, commanding First Panzer Army, remarked, 'no Russians in front of us, no supplies behind us'. Grimly prophetic, as his men plodding forward to Baku at the southernmost coastal point on the Caspian Sea at the foot of the Caucasus Mountains were soon to discover.

With less than a day's respite following the capture of Rostov, AGA struck at the retiring Soviet forces. Stalin's volte-face regarding 'no retreat' proved to be correct as unit after unit slipped out of the planned encirclement while rearguards conducted well-executed defensive operations among the maze of small rivers and villages. Nevertheless, by 27 July the Germans had moved forward some 60km. The front now ran from the mouth of the Don River for some 160km towards the lakes north east of Verkhne-Kurmoyarskaya. This position was held by North Caucasus Front's Fifty-First Army and Thirty-Seventh, Twelfth and Eighteenth armies of S Front. North Caucasus Front was also responsible for defending the Black Sea and Sea of Azov coastline as far as Lazarevsk at the western end of the Caucasus Mountain range.

From that point to the Turkish border coastal defence was the responsibility of the Trans-Caucasian Front. The Black Sea Fleet now had its HQ at Poti, some 100km north of Turkey. To simplify matters S Front was subsumed into North Caucasus Front, which was divided into two: the Don Group, Fifty-First, Thirty-Seventh and Twelfth armies, under General R.Y. Malinovsky, would cover Stavropol to the east; the Coastal Group, Eighteenth, Fifty-Sixth and Forty-Seventh armies led by General Y.T. Cherevichenko protecting Krasnodar to the west. Trans-Caucasian Front was ordered to raise defences along the Terek River and garrison the passes of the Caucasian range.

By early August the Axis forces had reached a line running from Belaya-Glina in the west, north east through Salsk to Proletarsk, roughly 120km south east of Rostov. And still the Soviets pulled back, reaching the line of the Kuban River at its Black Sea mouth east to the Terek River. Industrial equipment was evacuated from Maikop, Armavir and Krasnodar as First Panzer Army swung westwards to cut off the Soviet retreat from the port of Novorossisk, Krasnodar and Tuapse in support of Seventeenth Army's slowly moving infantry. Crossing the Kuban River, Axis forces took Armavir on 6 August. To the east the defences along the Terek River grew in strength as did the bridgeheads on its northern bank. To the west the Maikop–Tuapse line was held by men of the Twelfth and Eighteenth armies. During early August Axis troops closed in on Novorossisk and Tuapse and the Soviets sent forward units of the Trans-Caucasian Front to support their defenders. Unfortunately, the railways from Rostov to Baku were jammed with industrial goods, refugees and food stocks which made movement northwards well-nigh impossible.

To deal with local insurgents Stalin had dispatched L.P. Beria, his chief secret policeman, with several NKVD formations with orders to secure the rear of Trans-Caucasian Front from local uprisings. Almost immediately the NKVD and Red Army came into conflict as Beria refused to release more than a tithe of his men to aid the regulars. As this in-fighting sowed discord behind Soviet lines, AGA prepared for the next phase of its campaign. First Panzer Army would head eastwards towards Grozny then drive to the Caspian Sea coast in the direction of Baku, all the while skirting the lower reaches of the Caucasus foothills. Specialist mountain troops would capture the mountain passes. To the west Seventeenth Army would move out from its HQ at Krasnodar to the Black Sea coast where, having taken Novorossisk, it would march down the coast to Batum. It all looked so straightforward on a map.

Axis reorganization to achieve these aims went virtually unnoticed by Soviet intelligence as they were too preoccupied with their own internal power struggles and staff shuffling generated by Beria's malevolent influence. Indeed, Stavka representative Beria created, on 23 August, the Caucasian Range Operational Group which assumed control of the forces charged with holding the passes. Now the Soviet command structure in this region began to break down which naturally played into the hands of the Axis. On 21 August a combined force of 1st and 4th mountain divisions planted the swastika banner on the summit of Mount Elbrus, the highest peak in Europe. Infuriated by the speed of the enemy advance, Stalin raged at his commanders who had lost Maikop. By late August the Terek River line was under attack. Probing various points finally gave the Germans a foothold on the Soviet bank at Mozdok and here they began to develop a firm bridgehead. Kleist's panzers were within 100km of the oil fields.

To the west Axis reinforcements were shipped from Crimea into the marshlands of the Taman Peninsula to support the push for Novorossisk, which, after several days of vicious street fighting, was captured in early September. To protect Tuapse, 120km to the south, four rifle divisions were sent to support a small force of marines already in place. But despite everything the Führer was dissatisfied with AGA's progress and, on 9 September, List was recalled and Hitler himself took command.

The supply problem had been present from the first days of the campaign, fuel and food being airlifted to First Panzer Army and then distributed by camel in some cases. Nor did the Caucasian passes prove to be as easy a set of objectives as Mount Elbrus. Dogged Soviet resistance was, yet again, demonstrating itself capable of holding the increasingly thinly stretched Axis forces. The link point of AGA and AGB was the weakest position of all, and here the virtually isolated 16th Motorized Division patrolled the Kalmuck Steppe, an area of salt marshes, arid and featureless west of the Volga Delta and Astrakhan. Occasional brushes with similarly isolated Soviet forces were the order of the day in this surreal landscape for week after week.

However, the situation in the Caucasus was slowly slipping beyond even Hitler's long reach. The capture of Novorossisk was the high point of the Axis advance on their right flank. The Caucasian passes in the centre held and on the left the advance bogged down due to the solidity of the Soviet defence, the onset of bad weather and supply problems. It was thus obvious that the rush south by AGA had failed.

Therefore, when the Soviets unleashed their offensive to encircle Sixth Army and the subsequent relief expedition failed the likely fate of AGA south of Rostov became clear, it too was in danger of being cut off and destroyed. Operation Uranus was rapidly followed by Operation Saturn, which began on 16 December with the aim of liberating Rostov on Don, thus cutting AGA's escape route to the north west. Support for this operation was to be provided by Trans-Caucasian Front's own offensive with its Black Sea Group moving towards Krasnodar and Novorossisk, following which it would join up with S (formerly Stalingrad) Front around Rostov, which, it was anticipated, would fall to the Black Sea Group.

Unfortunately for Stalin, Hitler, bowing to the inevitable, had given permission during the night of 27/28 December for AGA to retire to the north west. Only a week later First Panzer Army's rear-guard lay 580km from Rostov while Yeremenko's S Front was within 280km of its goal, having moved out on 1 January 1943. First Panzer Army's retreat, in the face of poorly co-ordinated attacks by Trans-Caucasian Front's Northern Group (N Group, which became North Caucasus Front later that month), passed back over the Kama River. In an attempt to speed up the pursuit N Group detached two Kuban Cossack cavalry corps with a strong force of tanks to make for Armavir, 60km west of Stavropol. But by now winter gales were having a devastating effect on Soviet operations across the Caucasus, slowing pursuit and attacks to a grinding halt. Now it was the turn of the Soviets to be at the mercy of ever-extending supply lines, forcing them to rely on air re-supply as the filthy, muddy morass beneath their feet and tracks turned to the consistency of glue.

As January 1943 drew to a close Stavka revised its plans to trap AGA as reaching Rostov was proving considerably more difficult than anticipated. S Front's three armies, Second Guards, Fifty-First and Twenty-Eighth, were to co-ordinate their movements with the right flank of North Caucasus Front's Forty-Fourth and Fifty-Eighth armies and the Kuban Cossack corps. The aim now was to take Bataisk, south of the Don River below Rostov. A further two more of North Caucasus Front's armies, Ninth and Thirty-Seventh, would fight alongside the Black

Sea Group with the objective of isolating AGA's Seventeenth Army. Simultaneously, on 24 January, Hitler withdrew the remaining elements of First Panzer Army from Armavir to Rostov, a move it made with remarkably little loss as the Soviets were still regrouping.

Nevertheless, the Soviet advance on Rostov was inexorable and by early February the flanks of S and North Caucasus fronts had linked up south of Salsk. This united front now moved on Bataisk and Rostov. Fighting desperately, Manstein's Army Group Don (AGD) was unable to hold onto Rostov, which fell on 14 February. The remnants of First Panzer Army and other assorted Axis stragglers south of Rostov were subsumed into Seventeenth Army, which held a line from Novorossisk arcing through Krasnodar and meandering to the coast of the Sea of Azov south of Yeisk. As February drew on Seventeenth Army found itself under increasing pressure. On 4 February Soviet marines landed in the Axis rear near Novorossisk but made little headway. Krasnodar, capital of the Kuban region, was liberated eight days later, allowing Caucasian Front to advance along both banks of the Kuban River in an attempt to split the defences and drive on to the Black Sea. This endeavour failed as Seventeenth Army fell back in good order making good use of the resources freed up by the shrinking of its lines. By mid-February the Axis line ran for roughly 100km from coast to coast behind which lay the Taman Peninsula. Utilizing three small rivers and a couple of large villages and with its right flank anchored just south of Novorossisk into which supplies could be ferried, Seventeenth Army dug in firmly. Hitler had not yet abandoned his dreams of conquering the Caucasus and intended to hold on to the Taman position as a bridgehead for future operations.

AGA returned to the umbrella of AGS and Seventeenth Army became a separate command consisting of eight German and three Romanian divisions, initially commanded by General Richard Ruoff. In German military jargon it was referred to as the Kuban Bridgehead in keeping with Hitler's illusion of aggressive action in the future.

Following on from the fall of Rostov AGA headed out of the city towards the open lands of the northern Caucasus. An important source of food for the USSR, it was an area that Stalin was loathe to concede.

Very quickly the problems of supply became evident and any beast of burden was pressed into service, as is the case with these camels. Soviet destruction of the few roads and the rail network was to play havoc with the Axis supply plans.

Although the haul of Soviet POWs was much fewer than anticipated, many were perfectly happy to work for their captors. Considerable numbers were recruited for Caucasian units and served the Axis loyally to the end.

Very little ship-to-ship action took place in the Black Sea and therefore many of the Soviet sailors were deployed as infantry. Their fighting qualities were admired by their opponents.

German mountain troops make their way to reach the summit of Mount Elbrus, a prestige and propaganda move that left Hitler unimpressed, even threatening the unit commander with a court martial.

When the occasion presented itself the Soviets deployed armoured trains to provide mobile firepower. Often these were locally improvized, although the Red Army did have a small fleet of such trains.

Not all Soviet attempts to evacuate equipment by rail were successful, as this image shows. Anti-aircraft guns are clearly visible on this captured train.

Caucasians, possibly Chechens, ride out to volunteer their services to the Axis. Already in revolt against Soviet power, they fought alongside the invaders until it became obvious that their independence movement was being exploited.

Due to the on-going insurgency in the Caucasus NKVD troops were drafted in to maintain order both at the front and behind the lines. They were firm upholders of Stalin's policies and brooked no discussion or dissension.

Against the picturesque backdrop of the Caucasus range Soviet anti-aircraft guns drive along the old Georgian military road. The weapons just visible in the rear truck are anti-tank rifles.

An interesting image of a SdKfz 132. This tank destroyer consisted of a Russian 76mm anti-tank gun mounted in a box-like superstructure on a FAMO chassis similar to that of a Panzer II. The caption notes that they are taking up positions to forestall a Soviet tank attack in the Caucasus.

In the background the port of Novorossisk, in the foreground a German 37mm anti-aircraft gun deployed for firing at ground targets waits for a Soviet counterattack.

Romanian troops advance into a town in the Caucasus. By now these allied formations were wondering what they were doing so far from the areas that they had liberated from Soviet rule.

The lonely vigil kept by men of the 16th Motorized Division on the arid Kalmyk Steppe maintained the tenuous connection between AGA and AGB. the terrain was generally less welcoming than that seen here.

As the fog lifts so the frost and snow becomes visible as this German mountain unit falls back in early 1943. Retiring at the pace of the slowest pack animal, such units fought semi-continual rearguard actions.

The Soviet pursuit of AGA was often slowed by the need to clear well-placed minefields and booby traps. This rifle-mounted mine detector is the model VIM-210.

Soviet artillery chivies the Axis retreat along. This Model 1927, 76mm regimental gun went out of production in 1943.

Some Germans did not manage to reach the security of their own lines.

By the end of winter both sides were dug in and conditions began to resemble those of the First World War. Here a German peers cautiously over the lip of his waterlogged trench in the Kuban Bridgehead.

The focus of Stavka's attention shifted from the Kuban Bridgehead in early 1943 and the troops there regarded themselves as a forgotten army. Munitions provision was kept to a bare minimum, denying the gunners, for example, much opportunity of showing off their prowess.

# Chapter Five

# With Our Backs to the River

On 3 September Stalin had told Zhukov, 'the situation in Stalingrad is getting worse'. However, only nine days later it was even more desperate. On 12 September men of Yeremenko's Stalingrad Front took up positions along the urban defence line and the city was divided into three defensive zones, northern, central and southern. It was a timely move as on the following day the Luftwaffe and German artillery bombarded the south central sector of the city. Then, at 0800hr, the infantry and armour attacked. Stalingrad was some 30km long and 8km wide backing on to the bridgeless Volga River, the western bank of which was steep, overlooking the eastern shore. To the south, almost a separate entity cut off as they were by the Tsaritsa River that flowed into the Volga, lay two largely residential suburbs dominated by the immense bulk of the grain elevator building. This area was defended by Sixty-Fourth Army (General M.S. Shumilov) and covered the left flank of Sixty-Second Army, which was responsible for the central and northern sectors. These latter included, moving northwards from Railway Station No. 1, the main ferry landing quays, the 102m-high Mamayev Kurgan (from which the entire city could be seen), the colossal industrial plants, the Red October Steel Factory, the Barrikady Ordnance Works and the Dzerzhinsky Tractor Factory (now given over to tank repair and construction). Beyond this lay the suburbs of Rynok where town and country met.

Fourth Panzer Army struck at the southern end of the front as LI Army Corps attacked Chuikov's centre and both Soviet armies were speedily fully engaged. It was a simple pincer movement with Fourth Panzer Army attempting to drive along the bank of the Volga as LI Army Corps burst through overrunning the Mamayev Kurgan to effect a junction with the armour at the ferry quays, thus cutting the city in half and depriving Sixty-Second Army of its main supply line to the east.

From the south 24th Panzer Division, acting in tandem with 94th Infantry Division, pushed into the suburbs while 14th Panzer and 29th Motorized divisions headed for the river bank. At first Fourth Panzer Army made steady progress reaching the Volga in good time. However, during the course of succeeding days this attack lost momentum as the damage done to buildings provided excellent defensive positions for the Soviet infantry. Despite this advantage, Sixty-Second Army was cut off from Sixty-Fourth Army. But LI Army Corps was unable to connect with Fourth Panzer Army. Soviet marines and riflemen, of the 92nd Naval Infantry Brigade and 35th Guards Rifle Division respectively, fought to the death in and around the concrete monolith that was the grain elevator. German artillery was now dropping shells on the ferry quays with increasing accuracy.

In the centre LI Army Corps had made excellent progress capturing both the Mamayev Kurgan and Railway Station No 1. It was only the arrival, during the night of 12/13 September, of 13th Guards Rifle Division that prevented the loss of the ferry quays. The loss of the Mamayev Kurgan was more significant as from its summit observers could call in artillery strikes on both flanks of Sixty-Second Army, and therefore it had to be recaptured. Equally importantly, the ferry quays had to be defended. Men of 13th Guards were told off to recapture the railway station and the Mamayev Kurgan as Chuikov moved his HQ to a part-completed bunker near the Red October Factory's landing stages, close to several oil storage tanks. To add to his worries Chuikov was ordered to contribute men and armour to a planned attack tasked with relieving the city that would come from the north near Rynok. However, before this could take place a series of furious German attacks cleared the bed of the Tsaritsa River, Railway Station No. 1 and the grain elevator but most importantly the central ferry quays. The last week of September was a dreadful one for Sixty-Second Army. With most of the Volga crossing points now in clear sight of the Germans holding the central quays Chuikov's force's rear was under almost continual fire. The 284th Rifle Division was ferried in to recapture the central quays. As this night attack began the Germans themselves struck only to be driven back. The German push had been held and both sides paused to lick their wounds, count the cost and make what plans they could. With his left flank virtually destroyed Chuikov expected the next attack from the south. However, this was not to be as Paulus had decided to regroup his forces for an assault on the factory zone in the northern district on Chuikov's right flank. There Soviet engineers were busily engaged creating anti-tank ditches and minefields. Anti-tank mines were only a part of the supplies ferried across the Volga, and although much of this work was carried out at night, some, inevitably, had to be shipped during the hours of daylight under cover of smokescreens when possible. The sailors of the Volga River Flotilla manned gunboats, patrol boats and minesweepers, all carrying supplies as well as covering the motley assemblage of other craft that plied those hellish waters. The combined efforts of Chuikov's staff and the VRF administration rapidly established cargo priorities, schedules and traffic control when the Red October Factory's quays became the Sixty-Second Army's main supply point. Discipline concerning the unloading and storage of every type of supply was ferocious as every shell, bullet and bandage counted.

However, just as Chuikov's forces were about to assault the German positions on the Mamayev Kurgan Paulus' second series of attacks began at almost the same point.

German armour, upwards of 150 tanks and assault guns, struck at the Red October and Barrikady factory complexes. By the evening of the first day, 27 September, Sixty-Second Army was once again in dire straits, a relieving attack by Sixty-Fourth Army notwithstanding. Relief, in the form of the understrength 193rd Rifle Division, arrived on the west bank. These men headed straight for the Red October Factory, their path lit by the garish flashes of gunfire and German star shells. In this nightmare landscape small, well-armed Soviet assault groups retook much of what had been lost during the course of the day. Equally successful was a Soviet attack on the Mamayev Kurgan, which, although it did not recapture the peak, denied this vital piece of ground to the Germans, a success made possible by the infantry's blood and massive artillery support from batteries on the eastern bank.

North of the factory district German forces were making steady progress reducing the Orlovka Salient, which overhung their left flank. East of this point the Germans were moving into positions from which they could threaten the Tractor and Barrikady factories from the north. To counter this possibility reinforced units of 39th Guards Rifle Division, accompanied by a handful of tanks, moved to bolster the defence of the Red October Factory. Suddenly and unexpectedly a group of German infantry, men of 295th Infantry Division, reached the Volga's bank via a drainage channel. Heading south, they were ambushed by Soviet rear units and put to flight. Chuikov's position was, however, reducing by the day into bite-sized chunks and by early October measured some 14km in length by depths that varied from 300m to 2km. The Volga River itself measured roughly 1km wide and was continually raked by shot, bomb and shell.

During the first week of October the German attacks on the factories stepped up a gear. To counter this parts of two more Soviet divisions crossed the Volga along with some twenty T 70 light tanks. To stiffen his men's resolve, Stalin ordered that, 'Stalingrad must not be taken by the enemy and that part of Stalingrad which has been captured must be liberated.' Happily for Sixty-Second Army, a large German attack on the factories planned for 5 October was disrupted by heavy artillery fire from the eastern bank. A similar attack two days later was broken up by fire from Katyusha rocket launchers positioned on the river bank near Chuikov's bunker. Horrific as the Soviet losses had been, Sixth Army was also calling for 'fresh meat' to reinvigorate the assault troops whose officers were reporting declining morale in the face of such 'fanatical Russian defence'.

Once again, although the Germans had punched their way closer to the river they had not broken Sixty-Second Army. Thus, as Hitler's fascination with Stalingrad grew, so did the pressure on Sixth Army to deliver the prize. On 14 October Hitler ordered the suspension of all operations on the Eastern Front until the situation in the south and particularly that of Stalingrad was successfully resolved. Later that day the war diary of Sixty-Second Army recorded:

1130 left flank 95th Division smashed in.
1150 enemy has occupied stadium at Tractor Factory. Our units cut off inside and fighting their way out.
1525 Army HQ guard now fighting in battle.

These few terse sentences written in the heat of battle do little justice to the fighting qualities of the men involved. There had been three German infantry divisions, two panzer divisions and hundreds of guns, mortars and aircraft committed to the struggle for just a few square kilometres of wreckage that the factories now were. During the course of the first day the Soviets gave ground conceding the Tractor Factory, which forced Chuikov's HQ to relocate to the rear of the Red October Factory. As day and night blended into one with dust and smoke reducing visibility to almost nothing, Paulus increased the pressure. On 23 October a fresh German division, 79th Infantry, was flung against the defenders of the Red October Factory just as the Barrikady Factory fell. Men of the Barrikady's Worker's Militia had fought and died alongside their regular comrades, with only five surviving. Now German troops were within 400m of the river.

On the flanks outside of the city Soviet attacks were made in a frantic effort to distract Sixth Army from the factories. The value of these attacks is debatable but, nevertheless, from 29 October onwards German operations in the city itself began to wind down. As Goebbels' Propaganda Ministry crowed of victory *landser* in their increasingly chilly positions, within a grenade's throw of Soviet lines, knew the harsh truth. The Sixth Army would not have the strength to mount such a powerful succession of attacks again unless heavily reinforced. Across the line every hour that passed in relative tranquillity allowed men and munitions to be brought up for the nocturnal river crossing. Against incredible odds the Soviets had held on and now Russia's old ally, General Winter, was beginning his unstoppable march across the steppe.

For many German troops the first they saw of Stalingrad was a hazy smudge in the distance with shadowy buildings standing like ghostly fingers pointing to the sky.

But for the first arrivals at the northern end of the city the majestic spread of the cool Volga River to their left must have seemed like an oasis after the parched, dust-encrusted steppe marches of the summer.

Soviet heavy artillery was based on the eastern bank of the river to provide covering fire. Less mobile pieces such as this Model 1939 280mm mortar, built at the Barrikady Factory across the Volga, were ideal for such work.

The fight for air superiority over Stalingrad was intense. Stalin's son, Vasily, served in the area.

A German machine-gun team takes advantage of a Soviet barricade to provide supporting fire for advancing infantry.

Still dressed in their cotton summer uniforms, Soviet riflemen fire at a German attack. The long summer evenings and early dawns extended the fighting day to the limits of human endurance. The stress of such close-quarter fighting took a huge psychological toll on the men involved.

Advancing cautiously, a German infantry section approaches a relatively undamaged building in the southern sector of the city. The possibility that it was undefended did little to ease the tension these men must have been feeling.

The hulls of damaged T 34s on flatbed rail wagons on a siding outside of the roofless Tractor Factory. The armour plate would provide excellent cover for a sniper.

A Luftwaffe officer peers through the dust towards Stalingrad as his men move through the rubble. Just visible, centre right, is the vast bulk of the grain elevator.

As a nurse tends a badly wounded man others of his platoon engage the enemy. The structure behind which they are sheltering appears to be the stove of a wooden house long destroyed. Stalingrad's workers lived in buildings such as this which were burned out during the air raids.

Riflemen counterattack during September's battles for the city. Some areas appear to have remained remarkably unscathed throughout the campaign.

An assault gun and accompanying infantry pass a group of POWs. The devastation is obvious as is the dryness of the ground. The lack of clean water became increasingly problematic for both sides.

Defending the remains of another workers' settlement, as the vast housing estates were known. Soviet infantry took whatever cover they could find. The Red Army soldiers adapted to the street fighting more rapidly than their opponents.

Part of the marshalling yards at Railway Station No. 1. This objective changed hands frequently during the early days of the battle.

Anything that would float was used to ferry reinforcements to the west bank. Here men of the Volga Flotilla row infantrymen across the river. The unease on the sailors' faces is apparent as a daylight crossing was a virtual death sentence.

Fighting amid the destruction wrought by their own bombers became an increasing nightmare for the *landser*. With cover thus provided, a small Soviet unit could hold out for long periods and inflict severe casualties on their attackers.

Red Army engineers labour to build the alternative rail link between Moscow factories and the resources of the south.

As the weather grew colder and the fighting still fiercer so to did the steely determination of both sides to see the battle through to the bitter end. The Germans are discussing the point of best attack 'somewhere in the Factory District'.

A Luftwaffe anti-aircraft gun team prepares a cooked meal near their quadruple-barrelled 20mm weapon. The caption suggests this position is covering Pitomnik airfield, the base of *Jagdgeschwader* 3 'Udet'.

Soviet infantry developed the small group tactics that proved so lethally effective during the Stalingrad fighting. Each group was specifically trained in house-to house, room-to-room combat. Every man was assigned a role and a weapon type so that team work was essential.

# Chapter Six

# The Loaded Pistol

That Stalin, during the early weeks of Operation Braunschweig, remained convinced that Moscow was still the Germans' prime objective was unsurprising. The fighting west-north-west of Moscow from late 1941 into the spring of 1942 had created a large salient at the top of which was the city of Rzhev. Running south down the road and railway that formed the salient's spine were the towns of Sychevka and then Vyazma, the latter lying at the salient's base. The German defenders, Ninth Army, were led by General Walther Model under the supervision of AGC.

With the Soviet offensive capability worn down – having experienced such near success during March and April – it now rested with Model to clear the rear of Ninth Army of Soviet units isolated, but still full of fight and acting as bridgeheads for airborne incursions. As engineers supervised the strengthening of defences on all sides of the salient, Model's staff worked to prepare a strike force to carry out Operation Seydlitz – the clearing of the German rear. Operation Seydlitz began on 2 July with German forces moving to positions that controlled the obvious escape route along the Obsha Valley which took some four days. The targets of this operation were Soviet Thirty-Ninth Army and XI Cavalry Corps, both holding positions at the head of a precarious corridor some 28km long which connected them with Kalinin Front to the west of the salient. Thirty-Ninth Army was commanded by a former regular army officer who had transferred to the NKVD, General I.I. Maslenikov. Much of his combat career had involved fighting insurgents in Soviet Central Asia. Consequently, his present command had adopted guerrilla tactics when almost cut off behind Ninth Army during April 1942. With their escape route now denied to them, the Soviet formations were at Model's mercy. His next step was to split the Soviets up and destroy them piecemeal. Some five days into the operation both Soviet forces were combined into one under Maslenikov. There followed two weeks of ferocious fighting during which the defender's cohesion eroded steadily. With its command and control almost non-existent, the Soviet units began to break up, fighting innumerable small-scale actions amid the forests and fields of the region. Finally, accepting that there was only one possible outcome as his front was unable to provide support, General I.S. Konev (commander of Kalinin Front), under orders from Stalin, instructed Maslenikov and his force's military council to fly out of the pocket. With its commander and staff gone, the deputy commander took over leadership of the remaining 8,000 men who fought on for a further three weeks. Very few Red Army men managed to escape the encirclement, although several hundred joined local partisan groups.

The Germans officially concluded Operation Seydlitz on 12 July reporting, 'Victory in the summer battle of Rzhev.' Maslenikov was to resurface quite rapidly as one of Beria's close associates in the Caucasus.

As a result of Ninth Army's success the so-called 'Rzhev-Vyazma pistol' remained pointed threateningly at Moscow. To consolidate the position Model continued to upgrade the defences on all sides of the salient as it was still an obvious target for future Soviet operations. Unbeknownst to Model, he was to be granted just over three months' respite before the next serious onslaught.

However, all was not tranquillity around the Rzhev Salient during the summer of 1942. Zhukov, commanding W Front (facing the eastern flank of the salient), and Konev's Kalinin Front (facing the north and west of the salient) launched several, smaller attacks on Ninth Army, known by the collective term Pogoreloe-Gorodishche Operation, which were carried out by Thirtieth and Twenty-Ninth armies of Kalinin Front and Twentieth and Thirty-First armies of W Front. These two fronts between them disposed of almost one-third of the USSR's total strength in men, guns and aircraft and almost half of its armour. Therefore, it can be seen that Stavka did not consider AGC a negligible threat despite the situation to the south and in the Caucasus.

On 26 September Stalin ordered that both the Rzhev and Stalingrad areas would be subjected to powerful offensives with Zhukov overseeing the Rzhev attacks and Vassilevsky those to the south. The code name given to the Rzhev offensive was Operation Mars, scheduled to begin on 28 October, roughly two weeks before Operation Uranus around Stalingrad. However, October's weather was wet not frosty, as anticipated, therefore, the going was unfavourable and Operation Mars was postponed. Nevertheless, the orders were issued to put men and machines into place from 10 October. As Zhukov noted, 'The forces of Western Front's right wing and Kalinin Front's left wing are to encircle the enemy's Rzhev grouping, capture Rzhev and free the railway line from Moscow to Velikie Luki.' On the ground, therefore, W Front's Twentieth and Thirty-First armies, supported by Twenty-Ninth Army, would attack the German line between Rzhev and Sychevka, following which it would head north to Rzhev where it would link up with Kalinin Front's Forty-First Army. Kalinin Front would launch a similar series of attacks on the western flank of the salient, utilizing Twenty-Second as well as Forty-First and Thirty-Ninth armies and then unleash I and II Mechanized corps to complete the destruction of Ninth Army. In keeping with pre-attack tradition, officers were ordered to, 'Provide all personnel with a bath and clean [under] clothes.'

Due to the inclement weather both fronts began their attacks simultaneously on 25 November in the wake of powerful artillery strikes. Severe weather grounded almost all aircraft on both sides. W Front's Twentieth and Thirty-First armies hit XXXIX Panzer Corps along and north of the Vasuza and Osuga rivers outnumbering the defenders 5 : 1. However, Model's policy of ground clearance to provide good fields of fire paid off and very shortly dozens of burning Soviet tanks and hundreds of corpses littered the ground or glowed in the fog, which reduced visibility as much as the falling snow. Another of Model's policies, centralized artillery control, now proved its value as German shells tore Soviet infantry attacks to bloody shreds. Defending solidly constructed and well-sited bunkers, the men of 102nd Infantry

Division smashed the attackers of Thirty-First Army over the course of three days' brutal fighting. The Twentieth Army's attack fared equally badly but its 247th Rifle Division crossed the frozen waters of the Vasuza River and managed to establish a small bridgehead. It was into this tiny enclave that the mobile group of VI Tank and II Guards Cavalry corps were to be committed. These units moved up during the night of 25/26 November along two narrow roads but chaos ensued as the mobile group became mixed with other formations and a huge traffic jam built up. Finally, on 27 November, the mobile group went into action, tanks and cavalrymen valiantly battling towards the vital Rzhev–Sychevka road. The cavalry took horrific casualties but elements of three brigades made it through a gap torn by the armour just as it was closed by men of 78th Infantry Division. Nor had the bridgehead to their rear expanded sufficiently to allow for the artillery support they so desperately required. Consequently, Zhukov ordered them to break out towards the west. W Front's attack was, by 28 November, clearly faltering.

On the western flank Kalinin Front's Forty-First and Twenty-Second armies had made significant inroads. Bursting through German forward defences, they were threatening the heavily fortified town of Belyi and were, so Zhukov believed, about to charge into the German rear. On 26 November Forty-First Army's entire I Mechanized Corps was ordered up and within 24 hours had driven a wedge into the enemy's position some 30km deep by 20km wide. As one German officer recorded, 'The situation in the Sychevka-Rzhev-Belyi was exciting enough' (already without this development). It was at this point that Forty-First Army's commander, General F.G. Tarasov, miscalculated and began to commit his forces piecemeal to the capture of Belyi.

The secondary attack near Rzhev by the 80,000 men and 200 tanks of Thirty-Ninth Army had also made some good, early progress but, by 30 November, it too was bogged down short of the rail and road lines south of Rzhev.

After 5 days Zhukov issued orders to reinforce Twentieth Army with 200 tanks and withdraw the mobile group. What he was unaware of was that AGC was about to counterattack. The break-out attempt by the mobile group, this time to the east, ended in absolute disaster. Nearly all of the remaining 100 tanks were lost as were the majority of the cavalrymen – those few who survived fought on as partisans until early 1943. Soviet morale plummeted. Nor were the Germans in much better condition, 5th Panzer Division reporting, 'soon there would be complete apathy perceptible in all ranks due to the severe over stress caused by the lack of sleep, severe cold, insufficient supplies and incessant combat activity'. But soon the Germans were to hear good news that would raise their spirits. The fighting around Belyi was swinging rapidly in their favour. During the first week of December the arrival of 12th Panzer Division enabled the counterattack to go in. This developed against Forty-First Army's southern flank when 19th and 20th Panzer divisions came up attacking on 7 December. The Germans hacked through Soviet lines and within three days had encircled a portion, some 40,000 with over 100 tanks, of Forty-First Army, which promptly dug in waiting for relieving attacks from the army's main body.

Despite the fall off in the momentum of his forces' attacks Zhukov determined on one more push from the Vasuza Bridgehead. Reinforced with the fresh V Tank Corps and resupplied with various other armoured units from Stavka's reserve, Twentieth, Twenty-Ninth and Thirty-Ninth armies were to co-ordinate an attack from 11 December.

First, two rifle divisions attacked but were shot to pieces as they advanced across a 4km front, and tank support was similarly hammered. What progress was made was lost to furious counterattacks and within 2 days roughly 300 Soviet tanks had been lost. Infantry casualties are not reliably available. The Soviet position was, by this time, untenable and the encircled remnants, having destroyed their armour and heavy weapons, broke out to the relative security of the main Kalinin Front's line. Some 4,000 escaped.

Stalin had by this time decided to reinforce the successes of Operation Uranus and denied Zhukov further assets as Operation Mars was deteriorating into a bloody shambles.

The Rzhev Salient and Ninth Army had survived to fight another day but it was a costly victory and in some respects a futile one. In March 1943 Model was granted permission to pull out of the salient. Operation Buffel (Buffalo) was the name given to the evacuation, which was carried out with little loss of life or equipment. This much fought-over ground was further devastated as Ninth Army withdrew. By shortening the line considerably, Operation Buffel freed up a score of divisions that could be more usefully deployed elsewhere. Operation Mars was side-lined in Soviet history, its failure being greatly overshadowed by the events in the south where Operation Uranus proved a far more favourable planet of war for the Red Army.

Soviet tactics were developing slowly in terms of sophistication, the human wave of infantry being replaced by more efficient use of combined arms tactics. Artillery and armour, as seen here, were more prevalent than during previous operations.

Once again German communications efficiency proved to be a vital element in their speed of response to Soviet incursions. The heavily wooded terrain is evident here.

A German infantry officer briefs his subordinates during the summer fighting on the flanks of the salient.

Soviet riflemen offer support fire to the attacking formations.

A Degtyaryov Model 1928 machine gun covers a clear field of fire. An excellent, simple and reliable weapon, it was nicknamed the 'record player' due to the flat disc magazine.

The German defences around the perimeter of the salient were strong and underwent further development before Operation Mars began. The efforts made by the men who built them paid off during the offensive.

Red Army men cut off behind enemy lines frequently sought shelter with local families or offered their services to the partisans. The Germans conducted round-ups to flush out such men. The consequences for those guilty of hiding them were usually fatal.

A T 34 pushes its way through thick undergrowth. The terrain forced the attackers to stick to the roads making their line of advance easy to predict.

German infantry moves up to occupy recently won ground.

A well-camouflaged Soviet patrol blends in with the terrain. Patrolling in strength was common to both sides. The sub-machine guns the men are carrying were particularly effective in close combat where the rate of fire counted more than accuracy.

Partisan activity threatened German supply convoys to such an extent that it was necessary to provide them with armoured escorts, such as this Panzer II.

Close fire support is provided by this 50mm mortar. With a maximum range of 800m, it was an effective weapon and its light weight, 12kg, made it easily man-portable even in the more extreme conditions.

German fire control was centrally co-ordinated throughout the salient. This 150mm sFH 18 howitzer is just about to be moved to a less-exposed position as the fighting draws closer.

The strength of German defences can be seen in this anti-tank position. The 50mm Pak Model 38 appears to be in better condition than the ground nearby.

A less-well protected anti-tank position with an abandoned Marder II tank destroyer (*Panzerjager*). Armed with a Soviet 75mm anti-tank gun, re-chambered for German shells, it was a stop-gap measure that proved very useful.

A Soviet ML-20 152mm howitzer dating from 1937 points towards German lines from a heavily camouflaged position. With a range of over 17km, it was capable of reaching almost anywhere within the salient.

German infantry prepare to defend a second-line position. Model's order to clear fields of fire in front of the defences has obviously been scrupulously followed.

Trophies taken from a German rear position are inspected by a Soviet soldier. Unfortunately, the signpost above the door is illegible so the location is unknown.

When Operation Mars ended in Soviet defeat Model visited his troops to distribute medals. This image shows one such event in December 1942.

The Soviet follow-up to the evacuation of the Rzhev salient was cautious. German losses were negligible.

# Chapter Seven

# Isolation?

In September 1942 two events, separated by hundreds of kilometres but joined by fate, took place. In Germany General Fritz Halder had been dismissed from his post as Chief of the General Staff for suggesting to Hitler that Sixth Army's flanks were dangerously weak and presented the Soviets with an opportunity to encircle it as it was drawn deeper into the streets of the city. In Moscow General A.M. Vassilevsky, Chief of the General Staff, began to work on Operation Uranus, the code name for the Stalingrad counteroffensive, with General G.K. Zhukov. As the fighting for Stalingrad ebbed and flowed so the planning continued.

With the end of Sixth Army's third attempt to take the city, on 29 October, it became clear that Stalingrad was unlikely to fall unless something quite unexpected happened or Paulus' forces were heavily reinforced. Given that the latter was unlikely and the former in the lap of the gods, it depended on the leaders of the USSR and the Axis to decide the next move. Hitler was preoccupied with events in the Caucasus despite his frustration with Paulus' lack of achievement, and Stalin now merely waited for his subordinates' plans to unfold.

The Sixth Army lay at the tip of a large salient. It depended for its supplies on a single railway line that crossed the Don River at Kalach, which was itself only 80km from Soviet lines. To the left of Sixth Army was Third Romanian Army (General Dumitrescu) defending 130km of front, which included two well-established Soviet bridgeheads over the Don River, one at Kletskaya the other at Serafimovitch. A proposed German-Romanian effort to capture the latter had been cancelled by the Germans due to their focus on Stalingrad itself. Paulus' right flank was covered by General Constantinescu's Fourth Romanian Army whose line petered out vaguely to the south on the barren wastes of the Kalmyk Steppe where 16th Motorized Division patrolled. The only reserves covering this 650km front were 22nd Panzer and 1st Romanian Armoured divisions, both weak formations that constituted AGB's major armoured elements. The 29th Motorized Division, to the west of Stalingrad, was its immediate reserve. With German eyes focused on the minutiae of combat in the city streets and factories the brooding, wintry steppes held little of apparent interest — Sixty-Second Army's tiny enclave was all that mattered.

The Russian word *maskirovka* embraces camouflage, deception and misinformation, perfectly encapsulating the concealment undertaking carried out to prevent Axis intelligence gaining precious knowledge of the Soviet build-up along the flanks of Sixth Army.

The offensive would take the form of an ambitious pincer movement. The two initial thrusts were aimed to the north and south of Paulus' position in and around Stalingrad, through the thin defences of Third and Fourth Romanian armies. The northern thrust would be conducted by Vatutin's SW Front's First Guards and Twenty-First armies with Fifth Tank Army to follow up and exploit the breakthrough. Next in line was Rokossovsky's Don Front that would utilize Sixty-Fifth, Twenty-Fourth and Sixty-Sixth armies pinning German forces, north west of Stalingrad, and preventing them from supporting the Romanians on their left.

To the south Yeremenko's Stalingrad Front would engage and breakthrough Fourth Romanian Army with Fifty-First and Fifth-Seventh armies. The Sixty-Fourth Army on the front's right flank, where it connected with Chuikov's Sixty-Second Army, would prevent any German reinforcements from supporting the Romanians.

When the breakthroughs were achieved both pincers would meet up at the Kalach bridge, west of the city. Happily for Stavka, Paulus had ordered a further attack by five infantry divisions on the stubborn defenders of the factory district on 11 November. This effort came to nothing after just two days, only weakening Sixth Army further mere days before Operation Uranus was due to begin on 19 November.

Following an 80-minute bombardment SW and Don fronts attacked along a 320km line, and 3 hours later the Romanian position in front of SW Front broke and the Soviets committed armour and cavalry to exploit the situation. These and other mobile groups, sticking to the letter of their orders to avoid serious combat, raced into their enemy's rear with Kalach as their prime objective. Hitler ordered XXXXVIII Panzer Corps to intercept this thrust and link up with the Romanian armour. However, moving through the night communications with the Romanians broke down. The latter were ambushed by XXVI Tank Corps and sustained heavy losses during the early hours of 20 November. Simultaneously, XXXXVIII Panzer Corps moved north westwards to support isolated Romanian infantry units. Later that day Stalingrad Front began its attack, later than planned but with similar success, rapidly collapsing VI Romanian Army Corps and leading Yeremenko to committing his mobile exploitation forces. However, 29th Mobile Division's timely counterattack held XIII Tank Corps until it was sent south to cover the rear of AGA in the Caucasus.

To the south west Fourth Panzer Army was ordered to move westwards leaving Fourth Romanian Army to its own, limited, devices. It now became apparent to Hitler that this was a serious offensive and that its consequences could be, to say the least, problematic. Consequently, Field Marshal Manstein was ordered from Vitebsk to take command of the newly formed AGD. Manstein was instructed to stabilize the Axis position in the south and prepare a relief mission aimed at relieving the Sixth Army's 'temporary difficulties'. Confident that the Soviet attack could be defeated, Hitler issued a further set of critical orders. On 21 November Paulus was told that, 'Sixth Army will hold positions despite the threat of temporary encirclement . . . keep railway line open as long as possible. Special orders regarding air supply will follow.' In the discussions that followed Paulus, his staff and Luftwaffe officers concluded that such a massive airlift as Sixth Army would require was impossible during winter. As Sixth Army had six days' supplies Paulus returned to his command on 22 November and established his HQ at Gumrak airfield just west of the city. From this point he began to re-deploy his forces to carry out a break-out. Aware that trying such an operation during a savage Russian winter across featureless steppe with few defensible positions, Paulus, a cautious leader at best, waited on events and further orders.

At Hitler's HQ in East Prussia the Führer was to seal Sixth Army's fate. He was convinced by Luftwaffe commander Herman Goering that his aircraft could supply Paulus' forces. Therefore, on 23 November, Stalingrad was declared to be a 'fortress', with, 'the duty to . . . withstand a siege. If necessary they will hold out all winter and I shall relieve them by a spring offensive.' Inside the Stalingrad pocket preparations for the break-out continued and troops were withdrawn from forward positions in defiance of Hitler's earlier orders. On 24 November the Führer declared, 'Sixth Army will adopt a hedgehog defence . . . present Volga front and northern front to be held at all costs…supplies coming by air'. Paulus and his men were thus set in place, they were to make no break-out attempt and they were to hold out in a position with a perimeter of some 130km.

As Hitler and his commander debated their options the Soviets had not been idle. To the north west the mobile groups of SW Front were rampaging across the open steppe, brushing aside the Romanian's improvised defences. On 2 November XXVI Tank Corps captured the bridge at Kalach in a surprise attack that caught the German defenders completely unprepared. The bridge was intact and the position held until stronger forces arrived to occupy Kalach town on the following day.

Indeed, at 1400hr on 23 November advanced elements of the northern and southern thrusts met up at Sovetsky farm, just east of Kalach – the Soviet pincers had closed. Within this fragile ring scenes approaching panic were being enacted by disoriented Axis formations, 'people abandoned everything, they threw away weapons and equipment, vehicles fully loaded with ammunition, field kitchens and baggage wagons stood motionless in the road as men could move forward faster by unharnessing the horses and riding them'. To the north some 27,000 men of IV and V Romanian army corps laid down their weapons on 23 November. As the remnants of Axis units flooded towards the apparent safety of Stalingrad Paulus looked to his defences, which now no longer only could face east. Equally, the Soviets, having achieved the breakthroughs and link-up, now began to consolidate their positions. The outer perimeter of the Soviet line ran along the rivers Don, Chir and Aksai for roughly 320km to the south west of the city and faced west. The gap between it and the inner perimeter facing Sixth Army was approximately 30–50km. Quite remarkably, considering the close quarters at which they were fighting in the city, Soviet intelligence was completely in the dark when it came to estimating the number of troops encircled in and around Stalingrad. Whereas the Soviets believed that they had cut off something approaching 90,000 troops, the figure was well over 240,000. Their mistake was to have consequences for the Red Army's plans as the liquidation of Sixth Army was to be a longer drawn out affair than originally thought, although this did not become apparent until early December. The miscalculation became more obvious following the initial efforts to overrun the pocket, which began on 24 November. This task fell to Fifty-Seventh, Sixty-Second and Sixty-Fourth armies. Encircled as they may have been, the men of Sixth Army certainly had not lost the will or the means to fight and gave their attackers a bloody welcome during the course of the following two weeks.

As the war on the ground raged, overhead the airlift began on 23–4 November with JU 52 transports carrying the bulk of the supplies into two airfields, one at Gumrak, the other at Pitomnik. During the first week out of 350 tons of supplies flown in only 14 tons were food: more than 30 tons were fuel, some of which was destined for the fighter aircraft operating from Pitomnik which flew cover for the transports. The following week's results were similarly poor, only a fifth of the 500 tons per day arrived. In part the problem was one of distance. Tatinskaya airfield, from which the transports flew, was roughly 200km south west of the pocket's airfields. Consequently, the fuel carried by the transports was at maximum load to enable them to complete the round trip thus reducing the load of supplies they were able to carry.

Furthermore, the Soviet air power in the region was growing stronger and their fighter aircraft took an increasing toll of the lumbering transports. So high were the losses that bombers were pressed into service to supplement the JU 52s.

As the fighting around the Stalingrad pocket continued so did the operations on its external western perimeter. Romanian Third Army and a hodgepodge of German units had coalesced to form a defence line, under the command of General Karl Hollidt, along the banks of the Chir River. To Hollidt's right lay Fourth Panzer Army minus the bulk of its armour and some Romanian divisions from Fourth Army. Beyond them was the meagre screening force of 16th Motorized Division which still maintained a tenuous link with AGA and the embryonic AGD.

However, as Operation Uranus had succeeded it was now time for the Soviets to launch the greater encirclement that would drive south through Italian Eighth Army, south of Voronezh, pushing past Tatinskaya towards Rostov on Don. The aim was to encircle all of AGD thus ruining any breakthrough attempt by Manstein and sealing Sixth Army's doom along with that of AGA in the Caucasus. The code name for this undertaking was Operation Saturn. It was nothing if not ambitious and, under the prevailing circumstance, a not impossible task.

Regarding Sixth Army, the initial attempt to destroy it having totally failed due to its unexpected size and resilience, a separate plan was drawn up and submitted to Stalin on 9 December by Rokossovsky. The code name was Koltso (Ring) and its purpose was to break up the pocket by a series of three attacks and then destroy the smaller segments in detail. It was anticipated that Operation Koltso would be completed by 23 December. Stalin granted his approval for the Stalingrad end game on 11 December. But Manstein had not been idly kicking his heels at the HQ of AGD in Novocherkassk, he had been planning a counterstroke that aimed at relieving Sixth Army and restoring the Axis position in southern Russia and the Caucasus. Naturally, the Soviets had considered such a possibility, Zhukov and Vassilevsky privately concluding that the main Operation Saturn would have to be postponed and a smaller Operation Little Saturn take place to deal with any relief attack mounted by AGD. Thrust and counterthrust were about to break out across the windswept, snowy steppes south west of Stalingrad.

The last German attacks to break through to the Volga floundered amid the ruins of factories and offices, such as those seen in this neatly posed image.

Repairing the landing stages on both sides of the river was an on-going labour carried out by Soviet engineers in all conditions and in all weathers.

As the attacks petered out the Germans settled back to await orders. Here a group of gloomy, resigned infantrymen sit and read letters from home.

Maintaining the single rail line to Stalingrad was a continual job for the Germans. The Sixth Army's dependency on this supply route was critical. Therefore, when it was cut by Soviet troops in late November an air bridge was the only alternative.

Soviet infantry head for cover as they disembark on the western bank of the Volga.

Fighting in the factory district.

In the wake of a jet from a flamethrower Soviet infantry rush forwards to take advantage of the weapon's devastating effects. The flamethrower operator is standing in the foreground.

Preparing for another Christmas in the USSR. Despite the horseshoe and other good luck charms, it is unlikely that Helene ever saw her beau again.

Apathy slowly descended like a fog on many of the troops trapped in the *kessel* (cauldron), as the Stalingrad pocket was known to its inhabitants.

Inside the chemical works a tangle of pipes and equipment illustrates the difficulties of industrial zone warfare.

FW 200 Condor bombers were drafted in to supplement the JU 52 transport. With a payload of 6 tons the Condor was a useful addition to the air bridge's assets.

One of the anti-aircraft guns positioned around the pocket to interrupt the air supply route. This is a 72-K 25mm Model 1940 a/a gun which had a 2,000m ceiling of fire.

Supply 'bombs' waiting to be loaded aboard a He 111 bomber for delivery to Stalingrad. Dropped by white parachute, these canisters often fell into Soviet hands or disappeared from view in the snow. Moves to replace the white parachutes with red were too late to have an effect.

An iconic image from the opening barrage of Operation Uranus showing rockets flying over an artillery position.

Cavalry units formed an important part of the mobile exploitation groups that were pushed into Axis rear areas. Operating in conjunction with armoured units, the cavalry provided a source of mobile infantry when trucks would have to have relied on less available fuel than the hardy steppe ponies.

T 70 light tanks, part of an unidentified mobile group, pass an artillery position. The T 70 was armed with a 45mm gun. Unfortunately, the relatively light armour made it too vulnerable for tank-to-tank actions. The rear of a T 34 is just visible to the left.

Soviet artillery out on the steppe prepares to fire. This is a battery of ML-20 152mm howitzers. The crew shelters are just visible to the rear left where the stove pipes poke out of the snow.

Heroes of Stalingrad. General V.I. Chuikov inspects V.G. Zaitsev's sniper rifle. Both survived the battle and the war and are buried in the city where they fought.

Not all the German units retired on the city in haste or panic. Here one of the better organized formations withdraws in good order. The lack of camouflage and winter kit is shown to good effect here as the entire column is clearly visible.

A group of miserable Romanian POWs considers its fate. During the course of the next year many were recruited in the Soviet sponsored 'Tudor Vladimirescu' Infantry Division.

During the course of the Stalingrad campaign the Soviets slowly established air superiority over first the pocket and then the entire southern region. Pushed back to air fields further west, the Luftwaffe was forced to fly greater and greater distances to provide air cover for the transport fleet and the ground forces.

In an effort to disrupt Axis supply lines small units of ski-troops were despatched behind enemy lines to sabotage the track. Here one such group mines the line. Further west partisan units performed the same task to interrupt the flow of reinforcements from Western Europe.

# Chapter Eight

# **Near Collapse**

Somewhat more dramatically titled than operations Uranus or Koltso, the offensive to relieve Sixth Army was code-named Operation Winter Storm. Its purpose was to re-establish a corridor to Stalingrad for reinforcements and re-supply as the Führer was expecting Paulus to hold his keystone position on the Volga River as a base for future operations in southern Russia. Manstein had also drawn up a plan that would allow for Sixth Army to be pulled out should Winter Storm prove successful: known as Operation Thunderclap, it could only be activated with Hitler's approval.

Initially, Winter Storm was a two-pincer outflanking move, with one thrust from the north along the Chir River less than 50km from the pocket and the other from the south around the Kotelnikovo railhead, just over 120km from Sixth Army. However, as Fifth Tank Army kept up its attacks along the Chir River the German operation was finally mounted by the forces of the southern pincer only. Here stood LVII Panzer Corps, powerful in name but not in armour, having only thirty serviceable tanks, and two Romanian cavalry divisions. On 27 November the first of its reinforcements arrived, the 200 armoured vehicles of 6th Panzer Division. Literally jumping from the train into action, the division proceeded to destroy IV Cavalry Corps, a brigade of camel-mounted central Asian conscripts. As 6th Panzer Division completed its assembly and deployment Fourth Panzer Army moved off towards Stalingrad on 12 December. The speed of the Axis attack caught the Soviets unprepared. Within 24 hours 6th Panzer Division had advanced 40km and crossed the Aksai River. Then it rained and an unseasonable thaw mired the Germans down around the village of Verkhne-Kumsky. For three days the battle see-sawed around the village until the arrival of 17th Panzer Division, with powerful Luftwaffe support, restored the attack's momentum pushing it on to the next river line – the Myshkova. In the light of this Axis success Stalin acceded to Yeremenko's request for reinforcements and transferred Second Guards Army to his Stalingrad Front's command. However, blizzards held up the Guards' movement causing Yeremenko to fret that Sixth Army's tanks would break out towards the relief force, now within 60km of their objective. Consequently, Operation Koltso was postponed, although Rokossovsky was ordered to continue harassing Sixth Army with ground and air attacks.

The advanced elements of Second Guards Army began to arrive on the banks of the Chir River on 18 December, the day before 6th and 17th Panzer divisions established bridgeheads on the Stalingrad side of the Myshkova River.

But it was too late, Operation Little Saturn had begun along the front of Italian Eighth Army on 16 December. The first three days of Little Saturn went very badly for the Soviet Sixth and

First Guard armies, and they made little progress, losing thirty tanks in an unmarked minefield. Then, on 19 December, the Soviets broke through along a 48km front that led to SW Front freeing its mobile groups, which headed directly towards the rear areas of AGD. Their objectives were the isolation of Manstein's forces by the capture of Kantemirovno, Millerovo, Tatinskaya and Morozovsk, the latter pair being the main airfields from which the now creaking air bridge to Stalingrad began and the former two railway junctions crucial to AGD's communications to the west. On 19 December, with the Italians virtually surrounded and with no mobile reserves, the Axis position began to collapse and Vatutin was granted permission to expand Little Saturn into the original Operation Saturn concept. By 23 December Tatinskaya was under threat, and fell the next day. Although its loss was temporary and it was recaptured within days, it was no longer safe to use as an airfield and the Luftwaffe moved further to the west. The Soviet mobile groups' rate of advance was spectacular as they raced for their objectives virtually unopposed, but in doing so they began to outstrip the supply units therefore they paused to let their rear echelons catch up. This respite enabled Manstein to re-group but in doing so he effectively ended Operation Winter Storm. As General Rauss, commanding 6th Panzer Division, wrote of the order that pulled his men back, 'This signified defeat at Stalingrad.' In the city itself Soviet troops welcomed the onset of cold winds and hard frosts, indeed the Volga River finally froze to such a depth that it became possible to drive supply trucks across. The lack of shells now plaguing the Germans made the crossing a relatively pleasant excursion.

With its resources massively depleted and rations cut almost daily to dangerously low levels, starvation and illness became foes more dangerous than the Soviets for the men of Sixth Army. To erode German morale even further than the lack of food leafletting campaigns and propaganda broadcasts encouraged desertion, denying the belief held by Axis troops that POWs were shot on the spot and promising good treatment. Although there were instances of desertion and self-inflicted wounds, such events did not occur on a large scale despite the best efforts of German communists working for the NKVD.

On 26 December Paulus informed Manstein that, 'Bloody losses, cold and insufficient supplies have reduced the fighting strength of divisions severely.'

The New Year came and went and Paulus signalled, 'Army starving and frozen, have no ammunition and cannot move tanks anymore.' By this time AGD had almost retired to a line 240km west of Stalingrad. Now, therefore, was the time to start Operation Koltso. Part of this operation included the Red Air Force, which, by early 1943, had created a 50km zone around the pocket that, when combining aircraft and anti-aircraft guns, took an increasing toll of the German transports. However, it was the men on the ground who would carry out Operation Koltso and the plan was to develop in the following manner. The pocket was to be attacked from the south by Fifty-Seventh Army, the west by Second and Sixty-Fifth armies and from the north by Sixty-Sixth Army. The Fifty-Seventh, Sixty-Second and Sixty-Fourth armies were transferred to Don Front when the Stalingrad Front was disbanded, the whole to be commanded by General K.K. Rokossovsky and to begin on 6 January. Yeremenko took over S Front, already engaged in pushing back Fourth Panzer Army. To the north Golikov's Voronezh Front was ordered to attack Second Hungarian Army and then Second German Army, west of Voronezh itself. The battered but still effective AGD was to be dealt with by SW Front.

Rokossovsky asked for a four-day postponement of Operation Koltso, which was grudgingly approved by Stalin who was by this time desperate to conclude the fighting in Stalingrad and move on towards the Dnieper River and thus liberate eastern Ukraine. To speed matters up and conserve resources, Sixth Army was to be offered the chance to surrender. Terms were transmitted to Paulus on 7 January which included medical treatment for the wounded and normal rations. To reinforce the apparent hopelessness of Sixth Army's situation the message noted, 'you as commander ... fully realise that you have no real possibility of breaking the ring of encirclement. Your position is hopeless and further resistance can serve no purpose whatever.' The offer concluded with the bald statement that should it be rejected Sixth Army would be wiped out. Repeated on 9 January, terms were yet again declined.

Operation Koltso began at 0805hr on 10 January 1943 with a barrage that lasted for 55 minutes. A total of 7,000 guns, mortars and rocket launchers deluged the German lines and the succeeding rolling barrage moved ahead of the infantry and armour that attacked all along the perimeter line of the pocket. Within 48 hours the western nose of the German line, the Marinovka Salient, had been virtually eliminated along with two infantry and one motorized division. Axis troops streamed back into the apparent safety of the city itself.

Now Rokossovsky switched his main effort to Twenty-First Army. It was given the objective of Pitomnik airfield, the major entrepôt for the airlift, which fell on 16 January. However, by this time a further five infantry and two motorized divisions had virtually ceased to exist. Sensing victory, Rokossovsky denied his subordinates permission to rest and regroup, goading them to further efforts and specifying the last airfield at Gumrak as the new target.

As the tanks of Sixty-Fifth Army approached Gumrak the last aircraft flew off westwards bearing those officers deemed too valuable to lose. The thousands of sick and wounded lying around in the battered buildings received little or no attention, let alone food, which was now reserved for those still able to fight. Triage was operated beyond the ramshackle wards. Gumrak was taken on 23 January and the following day the Luftwaffe lost contact with its liaison unit in Stalingrad. Far to the west Hitler was already planning to recreate Sixth Army, assembling a skeleton staff to which evacuee officers were attached. Meanwhile, the first major collapse took place on 25 January when General Drebber surrendered with the remnants of his 297th Infantry Division. Other senior officers chose suicide or death in combat whereas Paulus appeared to be sinking into a state of torpor and nervous collapse. And still the agony of Sixth Army continued.

On 26 January armoured units of Twenty-First Army linked up with infantry of Sixty-Second Army, north of the Mamayev Kurgan. This move meant that the pocket was now divided into northern and southern sections. The northern section's units grouped themselves into positions held by XI Army Corps, which was dug in near the Tractor Factory under the command of General Strecker. To the south Paulus still commanded from his HQ under the Univermag department store on the city's Red Square. Desperate as the situation now clearly was, Sixth Army's staff still found the time to congratulate Hitler on the tenth anniversary of his coming to power on 30 January 1933. The Führer rewarded Paulus with a Field Marshal's baton just as Soviet troops began to filter into the city centre. Paulus surrendered 24 hours later, emerging into the full glare of daylight and the lenses of the waiting cameras of the Red Army press corps, brought to the scene to capture the moment of triumph for posterity. On 2 February the northern pocket also surrendered. Stalingrad had been liberated and the Sixth Army consigned to history.

Further to the north Second Hungarian Army's position had been breached and its units fell into confusion as command and control all but collapsed within three days of the initial attack on 12 January. By 27 January the Hungarians were surrounded along with the Italian Alpine Corps on their right: the Soviets counted over 85,000 POWs in this area alone to add to the 90,000 taken at Stalingrad. To avoid a similar fate, Second German Army was allowed by a temporarily chastened Hitler to withdraw from Voronezh. However, it was a much battered force that was only just capable of slowing the seemingly relentless Soviet pursuit. AGB and AGD seemed on the point of extinction and the path to the Dnieper River wide open.

A Panzer III pauses to consider its next move near a hamlet south west of Stalingrad. The large drum behind the turret carries extra fuel supplies.

A Soviet cavalry patrol scans the steppes for any sign of the enemy.

As well as Axis troops falling back to the west, locally recruited units of Cossacks, Caucasians, Russians and Ukrainians retired as fast as they could to avoid the inevitable retribution.

An NKVD propaganda broadcasting truck, several of which were deployed around the Stalingrad pocket's perimeter. They delivered messages varying from the horrific body count to the reading of captured letters from the Home Front.

A pause for communications and food for the crew of this Panzer III. The camouflage whitewash is wearing thin revealing the original grey factory finish.

The pace of the Soviet advance was sometimes held up by the lack of supplies, some of which plodded forward at a snail's pace and were prey for isolated and desperate Axis troops.

Horse power assists a bogged down German staff car. A large proportion of the troops caught in the Stalingrad pocket were not combat troops but administration and rear echelon soldiers.

Fully clad, men of a tank *desant* unit mount up and ready themselves for a bumpy ride into action.

An assault gun unit pauses to deal with POWs captured during the early days of Operation Winter Storm.

Soviet gunners move forward. The weather is clearly atrocious but at least they can ride on the tractor, limber and gun barrel.

A front-line observer, well-kitted out for his lonely and hazardous job, poses for the camera. The men of Sixth Army found it well-nigh impossible to dig defences in the solidly frozen ground and made use of former Soviet positions.

German anti-aircraft men KIA, December 1942.

A SdKfz 251 variant 10, armed with a 37mm anti-tank gun (here without the shield), leads a column of other half-tracks during Operation Winter Storm. The frozen ground made for good going but rapid thaws reduced progress to zero.

Operation Koltso aimed at the final destruction of the Sixth Army. The barrage that preceded it was intense. Here a 75mm gun prepares to fire.

Abandoned for lack of fuel, this SdKfz 232 is parked among hundreds of other vehicles in and around Stalingrad. Issued to reconnaissance units, the 232 was not best suited to the extremes of a Russian winter.

Some troops fought on, driven by duty or the dream of relief.

Field Marshal Paulus, with his general's insignia, shortly after the surrender. A German offer to exchange Paulus for Stalin's eldest son, a POW since July 1941, was rejected by both dictators.

It was not only the Axis troops that lacked winter camouflage, the Red Army was also short of these vital items of kit.

Using their own against them. This Soviet anti-tank unit has turned a captured PAK 75mm gun against its former owners. So much equipment was taken that such scenes were common.

The 'Glorious Dead' lay in undignified heaps waiting for burial in mass, unmarked graves outside the city they died fighting to capture. Many have been stripped of clothing and boots by the surviving civilians.

# Chapter Nine

# Recovery and Respite – Manstein's Gamble

As January 1943 drew to an end AGB was almost non-existent as a fighting force. The Soviet offensives had torn a 320km hole in the front line. Adrift in this apparent sea of Red Army units, the Axis formations did what they could to stem the tide. But there was more to come as Stavka now prepared to roll out the next phase of the winter campaign's operations. These plans were vastly ambitious, involving the destruction of the soon to be reconstituted AGS and then to be followed by an attack on AGC's position around Orel.

The dreadful situation of the Axis forces in southern Russia had led Manstein to the conclusion that there was but one way to defeat the Soviet offensives and restore the line – mobile defence, drawing the enemy to the limits of its endurance and supply lines onto ground of his own choosing where it would be opportune to counterattack. However, this flew in the face of everything Hitler regarded as good strategy. Almost to test the waters, Manstein requested permission to withdraw from Rostov and establish a defensive position along the Mius River, which covered his right flank down to the Sea of Azov.

On 6 February field marshals Kluge (commanding AGC) and Manstein were summoned to East Prussia to discuss the situation with Hitler. Kluge was granted permission to withdraw from the Rzhev salient and use the divisions released to bolster his right flank near to Second Panzer Army. Manstein put forward his ideas which, after much debate, were accepted. Returning to his HQ at Zaporozhe on the eastern bank of the Dnieper River, Manstein now had to wait for the arrival of reinforcements from Western Europe and their concentration, all of which would eat up valuable time while allowing the Soviets to plunge closer to the Dnieper River crossings.

The Soviet commanders were not sitting and awaiting developments as they savoured their victory at Stalingrad. Having smashed through the Hungarians, Golikov's Voronezh Front now prepared to launch Operation Star, a three-pronged attack on Kharkov, the fourth most important city in the USSR and the centre of the Donbass industrial region. Operation Star began on 2 February. SW Front, commanded by Vatutin, had already started its own offensive, Operation Gallop, on 25 January. This aimed to, 'prevent an enemy withdrawal on Dnepropetrovsk and Zaporozhe', both major crossing points on the Dnieper River. Vatutin's force consisted of four armies, from north to south, Sixth, First and Third Guards and Fifth Tank armies, supplemented by 300 aircraft and a mobile group with 137 tanks, 3 rifle divisions and ski battalions.

Golikov's first phase objectives were directed toward Kursk to the north, Belgorod in the centre and Kharkov to the south. The two latter cities were situated on the western bank of the upper Donets River. The Sixtieth Army was ordered to march on Kursk and Fortieth Army to liberate first Belgorod and then push on towards Kharkov, a move co-ordinated with SW Front. However, the strain of the winter's fighting was beginning to tell as Soviet units were slow to reach their jump-off points due to physical exhaustion, damaged infrastructure and supply problems. The attack towards Belgorod began on 3 February and the Donets River line the following day, while to the north Sixtieth Army headed confidently towards Kursk. Crossing the Donets line proved to be easier said than done. Following six days of vicious fighting Fortieth Army incurred heavy casualties, lost many tanks and its stocks of ammunition were severely depleted. However, SW Front's Third Guards Army had crossed the Donets River south of Kharkov and, with the fall of Belgorod on 9 February, just 24 hours after the liberation of Kursk, Vatutin and Golikov could focus on their joint attack on Kharkov.

The surrender of Sixth Army at Stalingrad on 2 February followed by this further series of Axis disasters had led to a rapidly expanding gap between AGC and AGS which generated the probability of yet further horrors for Hitler and his allies. By midday on 15 February Kharkov was under threat from the west, the north and the south east. Defended mainly be units of the SS Panzer Corps, the city looked ready to fall and with it another huge chunk of Manstein's diminishing command. Kharkov was liberated on 16 February but did not yield the anticipated bag of POWs as SS *Obergruppenführer* Paul Haussser, commander of the SS Panzer Corps, retreated from the city in defiance of all orders. By this move he saved the SS Panzer Corps' three Panzer Grenadier divisions, Leibstandarte, Das Reich and Totenkopf for future operations.

This near-disaster prompted Hitler to fly to Zaporozhe to discuss the situation with Manstein in person. His timing was excellent as Manstein had completed his planning for the counterblow he wished to choreograph. As the Soviets were now within 20km of Dnepropetrovsk and 60km of Zaporozhe time was of the essence, for the Red Army's mobile groups were proving their worth and probing towards their objectives with determination and confidence. Happily for Manstein, Stavka had misread his westward redeployment. As the official Soviet history admitted later, 'Both the S. W. Front command and Stavka were led to believe from the enemy's retreat from the lower Donets to the Mius and the transfer of his armoured and motorised divisions from Rostov . . . that the Germans intended to . . . retire behind the Dnieper'.

The plan Manstein put before the Führer comprised three stages.

Stage one involved the SS Panzer Corps attacking the salient formed by SW Front's right which threatened Dnepropetrovsk and Zaporozhe from the north, while XLVIII Panzer Corps (the main element of Fourth Panzer Army) struck the southern flank of the salient thus pushing it back towards the Donets River.

In Stage two the same panzer formations would regroup to strike at Voronezh Front, recapturing Kharkov and Belgorod and re-establishing the line along the upper reaches of the Donets.

The final stage brought in AGC's Second Panzer Army advancing from the north and linking up with Manstein's armour to re-occupy Kursk and thus straighten the line south of Orel down to the Sea of Azov along defensible positions that included several major waterways.

Even as the Germans positioned their forces for what was known as the Donets Campaign, the Soviets continued to misunderstand their intentions. By this time both Vatutin and Golikov's units were reaching crisis point in terms of re-supply and reinforcement. Indeed, Golikov shouted his army commanders down when they appealed for time to pause and consolidate.

Having given Manstein the go-ahead, Hitler and his staff returned to Germany on 19 February when Soviet cavalry was a mere day's ride from Zaporozhe. The next morning the senior intelligence officer of S Front reported, 'solid enemy columns were pulling out of the Donbass'. Vatutin ordered his mobile group commander, General M.M. Popov, to keep advancing as the Germans were, apparently, on the run. Later that same morning, 20 February, the German armour struck Popov's flanks and the Soviet Sixth Army that was moving up in its wake. The next day Popov requested permission to pull back as his remaining twenty-five tanks could do little against overwhelming air and ground attacks. This plea and a similar request from Sixth Army were both refused by Vatutin who remained convinced that the Germans were retreating. Indeed, Sixth Army was categorically ordered to take Dnepropetrovsk even as its flanks were being chewed away. The XXV Tank Corps tried to obey an order to capture Zaporozhe but ran out of fuel 15km from its objective and was cut off by units of XLVIII Panzer Corps. Yet, such progress only encouraged Stavka to egg S Front into crossing the Mius River despite horrific losses in the face of stout defence.

However, events now overtook even Moscow's wishful thinking as Popov's main force was driven back and the threat to Vatutin's flanks became very apparent, furthermore Sixth Army was in real danger of encirclement.

To relieve Vatutin Golikov was ordered to send Sixty-Ninth Army and Third Tank Army to strike at the German attackers in the flank but due to the slowness of their movements they arrived too late to offer much support. As a result, Third Tank Army was placed under the command of SW Front and Golikov lost control of his best armoured asset. But any hopes that Vatutin may have lodged in this reinforcement was shattered when it was caught deploying, first by a series of Stuka attacks followed up by tanks and ten days later this battered force was itself encircled.

During the last week of February it became obvious to Manstein that stage one of his plan was reaching a successful conclusion and the main threat to the Dnieper crossings was being driven back. But now he had to face another worrying development, the early onset of the thaw, creeping up from the south and threatening to engulf his mobile formations in a sea of mud reducing their movements dramatically. Nevertheless, by 3 March, Vatutin's entire right wing was back on the eastern bank of the Donets River and furiously digging in. The next day AGS's armour began stage two of the campaign – the assault on Kharkov and Voronezh Front.

The Leibstandarte and Totenkopf divisions swung to the east of the city, while XLVIII Panzer Corps moved up from the south. By 10 March SS tanks had cut the Kharkov–Belgorod road and their panzer grenadiers were pushing into Kharkov's eastern suburbs. Remarkably, while his left flank was thus engaged, Golikov's right and centre were still pushing forwards. The Soviet units caught in Kharkov were not about to surrender meekly and the SS found itself involved in a bloody, ferocious series of street and house-to-house fighting. Eventually, the SS took the city's Red Square and the last action, in the Tractor Factory, ended on 15 March.

By now the scale of the crisis facing the Red Army's forces in the south was clear. Indeed, the possibility of an armoured thrust southwards from AGC was considered to be inevitable. Therefore, on 12 March, Rokossovsky's Central Front was ordered to send Twenty-First and Sixty-Fourth armies to support First Tank Army and prevent any such operation by AGC.

It had also been decided to pull back units of Voronezh Front's central and southern sectors to the eastern bank of the upper Donets River and to evacuate Belgorod, which was re-occupied by the Germans on 18 March. This event brought stage two of the German plan to a conclusion.

As Soviet reinforcements poured into the salient now firming up around the important rail junction at Kursk and the thaw slowing movement to a crawl, it was time for Manstein to reassess stage three. Nor was it only the enemy to his front that gave pause for thought. Trapped behind the Axis line were thousands of Red Army men, all looking to avoid capture and probing for a route back to their own lines. Such units were often large, determined and well-equipped and therefore it would be necessary to clear the rear of such stragglers before committing to further advances. Reluctantly, Manstein concluded that it would be prudent to postpone the drive on Kursk until such time as his rear areas were put in order and the supply lines brought up to an efficient, dependable level.

Despite not achieving its final objective the Donets Campaign had restored the front and inflicted a major setback on an over confident Red Army. Stalin understood that, once again, his plans had been too ambitious and that the Axis would remain east of the Dnieper River for longer than anticipated. Manstein's finely calculated throw of the dice had paid off.

To the north other front realignments were underway: the Demyansk and Rzhev pockets were both evacuated and the divisions thus released used to bolster positions elsewhere. The second Axis summer campaigning season in the USSR had ended in failure on a spectacular scale and the loss of men and materiel inevitably limited Hitler's options. What the Führer would decide to do during the summer of 1943 remained to be seen.

Out on the featureless, snow-bound steppes a group of German infantry maintain a lonely vigil. The fragments of dozens of Axis units, shattered by the Soviet offensives, were desperately trying to evade capture or retaliation by vengeful locals by making their way west. Outposts such as this were often the first sign of hope.

During the winter campaign the Soviets deployed dozens of batteries of Katyusha rocket launchers to add weight and horror to the artillery barrages. An unsubtle but effective weapon, it was nicknamed the 'Stalin Organ' by those who felt its effects.

Reinforcements from Germany and the occupation forces elsewhere arrived in the USSR often well-equipped for the harsh climate. However, partisan activity along the railway network leading to the front caused unexpected delays.

Soviet infantry cross a river that is beginning to thaw under the remains of a railway bridge. The retreating Axis forces had carried out a scorched earth policy thus creating huge problems for Soviet supply units.

A German machine-gun team watch and wait for the first signs of any Soviet troops. There were many gaps in the line that were only covered by ad-hoc formations. Sometimes a platoon would be responsible for patrolling several kilometres.

A column of T 34s rolls proudly into Kharkov's Red Square. This central area of the city was a showpiece of Constructivist architecture and boasted the tallest building in the USSR.

An interesting event occurred during the fighting around Kharkov between 8 and 9 March. The 1st Czechoslovak Independent Field Battalion raised in the USSR from refugees and POWs went into action for the first time. Commanded by Ludvik Svoboda (later President of Czechoslovakia), this small unit earned the respect of their Soviet allies by 'tenaciously defending their positions'. During the course of the next eighteen months it expanded to corps strength. As can be seen, all ranks dressed in a mixture of British and Soviet kit.

The increase in temperature that the thaw brought was outweighed by the ghastliness of conditions underfoot, as can be seen here. The sub-machine gun appears to be an MP28/11.

Although many of the armoured formations on both sides were motorized, the Axis had lost many of its vehicles as they were unable to cope with the the climatic conditions. Therefore utilizing local breeds of horse and farm vehicles was a widespread practice.

A German mortar team that was unable to withdraw quickly enough paid the price.

When the infantry of both sides were clad in their winter camouflage suits it was, in the heat of battle, difficult to identify friend from foe. Therefore, the Germans adopted a red stripe on each arm as a marker.

Each Soviet mobile group included several battalions of ski-troops. These specialists in winter warfare travelled fast and light and were expected to carry out reconnaissance missions that would have been difficult for other troops.

Infantry follow cautiously behind a Stug III during the advance on Kharkov. These vehicles proved their worth time and again.

As they fought their way back across ground they had lost not long ago, the Axis forces encountered reminders of the recent retreat. It was sometimes a simple enough task to restore vehicles abandoned for lack of fuel to good working order.

German scouts pose for the camera before the onset of the thaw.

Soviet infantry move their M1910 Maxim machine guns to better positions. In such conditions the narrow wheels proved less of an asset on frozen ground.

The lack of camouflage indicates little fear of air attack. The Germans are preparing to fire their 172mm Mortar K-18 in support of an attack by XLVIII Panzer Corps. Moving such a large weapon rapidly was well-nigh impossible.

Soviet cavalry of an unidentified unit belonging to SW Front go through their paces for the camera. Nevertheless, they had fought with efficiency and deadly effect against retreating, disorganized units west of Stalingrad and were still a sight to put fear into the hearts of cold, hungry and demoralized infantry.

By the end of March 1943 the panzer forces on the Eastern Front were worn down to a shadow of their former power. This command tank, a panzer III, shows all the wear and tear of weeks of continual movement and action. When the thaw reached its height the armoured troops of both sides took a well-earned breather and re-built their strength for the forthcoming summer campaign.